Knowledge

Central Problems of Philosophy

Series Editor: John Shand

This series of books presents concise, clear, and rigorous analyses of the core problems that preoccupy philosophers across all approaches to the discipline. Each book encapsulates the essential arguments and debates, providing an authoritative guide to the subject while also introducing original perspectives. These works by an international team of authors aim to cover those fundamental topics that, taken together, constitute the full breadth of philosophy.

Published titles

Free Will
Graham McFee

Universals
J. P. Moreland

Forthcoming titles

Action
Rowland Stout

Paradox
Doris Olin

Analysis
Michael Beaney

Perception
Barry Maund

Artificial Intelligence
Matthew Elton & Michael Wheeler

Relativism
Paul O'Grady

Causation and Explanation
Stathis Psillos

Rights
Jonathan Gorman

Meaning
David Cooper

Scepticism
Neil Gascoigne

Mind and Body
Robert Kirk

Self
Stephen Burwood

Modality
Joseph Melia

Truth
Pascal Engel

Ontology
Dale Jacquette

Value
Chris Cherry

Knowledge

Michael Welbourne

McGill-Queen's University Press
Montreal & Kingston • London • Ithaca

ISBN   0-7735-2301-4 (bound)
ISBN   0-7735-2305-7 (paper)

Published simultaneously outside North America
by Acumen Publishing Limited

McGill-Queen's University Press acknowledges the financial support of
the Government of Canada through the Book Publishing Development
Program (BPIDP) for its activities.

National Library of Canada Cataloguing in Publication Data

Welbourne, Michael
        Knowledge

(Central problems of philosophy)
Includes bibliographical references and index.
ISBN 0-7735-2301-4 (bound).—ISBN 0-7735-2305-7 (pbk.)

        1. Knowledge, Theory of. I. Title. II. Series.

BD161.W428 2001   121   C2001-903263-3

Designed and typeset by Kate Williams, Abergavenny.
Printed and bound by Biddles Ltd., Guildford and King's Lynn.

Contents

Introduction

This book is about KNOWLEDGE. More specifically, it is about the very idea of knowledge and its importance in the lives of human beings. That makes it, in the proper sense, an essay in epistemology (Greek for theory of knowledge). But epistemology has come to be practised and even understood, more often than not, in a rather narrow and quite special way. A typical modern definition goes like this: "the part of philosophy which discusses the desirable qualities of beliefs, such as justification, rationality and coherence and the ways in which we can acquire beliefs with these qualities, such as by reasoning and gathering evidence" (Morton 1997: 225). This book is not primarily concerned with issues like these, although it will inevitably touch on some of them; one of its central ideas is that, although such issues are undoubtedly important, they are not central to our understanding of the nature of *knowledge*. It can hardly escape notice that the definition is all about *beliefs*.

Perhaps the idea is this: a belief, provided it has the right constellation of desirable qualities, *is* knowledge. The constellation must presumably include truth, since the most obvious fact about knowledge in most people's eyes is that you can only know that P if P is true. But truth alone is not enough. I might believe that the university library is open this evening (Saturday) and I might be right; that is how it has always been during university terms. But suppose that, unbeknown to me, the university council had decreed, for reasons of economy, that it should now close on Saturday evenings; and suppose, furthermore, still unbeknown to me, that in response to student protests the vice-chancellor, exercising special powers, had ruled that it be opened *this* Saturday evening, the last Saturday before exams. Here it seems like a lucky accident that my belief happens to be true; and many people would jib at the idea that a belief which is only true by chance could ever count as knowledge. If we go along with this intuition, it looks as if there must be something else in the constellation of desirable qualities for a belief to count as knowledge, something that will exclude luck.

That may be no easy thing to find. Ever since antiquity, philosophers have been good at inventing reasons why we might be wrong, even about things we feel most sure of and think we know. Indeed, the ancient sceptics thought that their arguments, which were revived at the dawn of the modern age by Descartes (1596–1650), among others, were powerful enough to make all our beliefs uncertain. So, in their eyes, it's always going to be a matter of luck if a person commits herself to a belief that is actually true, and it will never be possible for her to confirm beyond all doubt that it is true. Better by far, they thought, to give up altogether on believing things. That policy, however, seems barely intelligible. It has been far more usual for philosophers, especially since Descartes, to try to find a strategy that can deflect the power of sceptical arguments and exclude mere good luck. So perhaps we need to include in the constellation of desirable qualities which might qualify a belief as knowledge some feature or set of features that will achieve this end.

There is a huge literature that explores these ideas, and in fact it has become quite common to refer to accounts of knowledge which develop them as "traditional". Characteristically, these accounts maintain that if you know that P, three things have to be true:

1. You believe that P.
2. P is true.
3. Your belief that P has some specially valuable status-conferring feature like being justified or obtained by a reliable method or whatever – something, at least, that excludes or at the very least minimizes the chances of its being wrong.

For this reason, accounts of knowledge along these lines have often been called "tripartite analyses". I shall also sometimes refer to them as "belief-theoretical analyses", since they typically assume that belief is the core component of knowledge. The problem that has dominated epistemology over most of the past half century has been the problem of working out what exactly the status-conferring feature mentioned in the third clause might be. A small industry has developed, cooking up counter-examples to discredit each newfangled version of the all-important third clause and then refashioning it to secure it against further counter-examples. The problem of finding the right formula, however, has proved to be singularly intractable and no consensus on its solution has appeared. Nevertheless, this style of analysis has largely prevailed over alternative approaches to the philosophy of knowledge; actually it made its first appearance in antiquity, in the writings of Plato (4th century BCE). It's stretching a point, however, to call it "traditional". Plato never committed himself to it, and in some of his most celebrated writings he is, in fact, very strongly committed to a view of knowledge that is completely at odds with it, a view that radically opposes knowledge and belief. Many philosophers since his time have followed him in this. It is really only relatively recently that the fashion for belief-theoretical analyses has largely occluded other ways of trying to understand the nature of knowledge. I believe that the belief-theoretical approach is seriously mistaken, but I shall try to make its attractions clear and, in Chapter 3, describe some of the more serious difficulties which it has to negotiate.

Another idea. Perhaps our typical definition of *epistemology* was never even intended to underwrite a definition of knowledge. Surely it wouldn't stretch things too much to take the word *epistemology* to refer quite generally to the study of our representations of how things are. Perhaps the thought is that all that really matters philosophically is that we get a correct account of the desirable qualities of beliefs – those qualities, whatever they may be, which will make our beliefs more likely to be true; whether they are thereby qualified to be called *knowledge* is only of minor importance. Given the tortuous and overblown character of many of the tripartite analyses on offer, and given the lack of consensus about them, it would be entirely understandable that some people should find this approach attractive. After all, why should we care about honing a precise definition of *knowledge*, correct to the last iota, one that will fit every case we should recognize as knowledge and exclude every case we should not? What turns on getting the detail exactly right and, anyway, what reason is there to suppose that there is one uniquely correct analysis to be found? What really matters to us, so it may be said, is our beliefs. It is important that they be true because they are what guide our actions. If I want some honey and believe there is some in the larder, then, other things being equal, I will go and look in the larder. Assuming I want my action to be successful, I had better take steps to ensure, so far as I can, that my belief is true. But what more could I reasonably want than a belief that is true and that may help me to succeed in getting what I want? So would it not be better, more to the point, to forget about knowledge and the bundle of intractable problems it seems to generate, and concentrate instead on the question of how to maximize the chances of a belief's being true?

A number of philosophers have adopted this stance and I have some sympathy with it. It seems a natural reaction to the more Byzantine developments in the philosophy of knowledge, and the questions it examines are clearly important. But this is not the approach I take in this book. This book is written in the conviction that the concept of knowledge really does matter. If it were possible to explain the meaning of sentences in the form "A knows that P" completely, as tripartite analysts suppose, in terms of truth, belief, and justification (or reliability, coherence, appropriate aetiology or whatever), there is a sense in which the concept of knowledge would not matter. Whatever could be said, using the word *know* or its cognates could be said without it, although no doubt at some cost in circumlocution; still, in principle, the circumstances which we describe using the vocabulary of knowledge could be described in terms of belief. Against this, I maintain that whatever role the concept of knowledge plays, it is not one that could be played by the concept of belief, however embellished. I hold, as Plato most famously held in the *Republic*, that the concepts of belief and knowledge are, in fact, categorially different. And I hold (this will sound cryptic but it will be explained in due course) that the aspects of human life from which the concept of knowledge arises, and in association with which it has many of its leading uses, are among the most characteristically human and important of all.

The aspects of human life I have in mind here are those involved with what philosophers often refer to as "testimony", although this is a rather portentous word for something ordinary and common.

It is philosophicalese for telling people things. The later chapters of this book are very largely concerned with testimony and its reception. It is unusual, although not unprecedented, to find this subject featuring centrally in a book about knowledge, but I think the topic is of the first importance. There are two main reasons for this. The first is that a vast amount of what we *call* "knowledge", and certainly a vast number of our beliefs, even, I daresay, a preponderance, are obtained from the say-so of other people: teachers, textbooks, newspapers, conversations with friends and relatives, and so on. How else, for example, do I know who my natural parents were? Or where I was born? Or what my paternal grandfather did for a living? In fact it only needs a little reflection to see that nearly all my "knowledge" about geography, history, science and current affairs, and even quite a lot about *myself*, derives from what I have been told either orally or in the things I have read. This being so, it seems amazing that testimony has not, on the whole, featured prominently in the writings of epistemologists, whether or not they are of the *knowledge*-analysing persuasion. In part, this book aims to redress this neglect of testimony and the bundle of problems associated with it. The subject should be of central interest to epistemologists of whatever persuasion.

But there is another, even weightier, reason why I think testimony is of special importance in the philosophy of knowledge. As I hinted just now, I hold that the way to achieve a correct understanding of the concept of knowledge is through understanding its connection with testimony. The development of that thought will involve us in a detailed discussion of testimony itself. How does it work? How does it come about that often a hearer, on hearing a speaker make an utterance of a certain sort whose content is P (or, of course, on reading such an "utterance"), ends up believing that P? The explanation of this simple fact is not itself simple. I hold that it will reveal a deep connection between testimony – the means whereby we come by so many of our beliefs – and the very idea of knowledge. The theory I am going to put forward may well prove to be contentious. It is certainly radical. Since I believe it to be true, however, and since I believe that the point is of the first importance, I make no excuse for presenting it in what is intended to be an introductory book. The least that can be asked of such books is that they should be as true as the writer can make them. And anyway, whoever said that introductory books should be uncontentious, or that the people for whom they are intended should not be exposed to controversy? That is the very stuff of philosophy.

The plan is this. In the first two chapters I use Plato to introduce the subject. A. N. Whitehead is said to have remarked that the whole of Western philosophy is a series of footnotes to Plato. There is a lot of truth in this, particularly so far as the philosophy of knowledge is concerned. In Chapter 1, I discuss some important issues about knowledge which Plato was the first to introduce. In Chapter 2, I review his main discussions about the nature of knowledge. In Chapter 3, we come to the modern age. I describe the "traditional" approach, the attempt to develop an analysis of knowledge as a species of specially qualified belief, and I examine a nest of problems associated with that attempt.

The focus then changes from analysis, and in particular the attempt to list the separately necessary and jointly sufficient conditions for an individual's knowing that P, to a discussion of the role of the concept of knowledge in human life. Chapter 4 prepares the ground for this project. It reminds us that the concept of knowledge is not only used to refer to the mental states of individual human beings but is also used to refer to something that is publicly available, something that can be communicated and taught to other people. It is in this connection that the idea of testimony, of telling one another what is what, becomes prominent. Testimony, broadly understood, is *the* way by which knowledge is made public and shared. Chapter 5 is largely about Hume (1711–76). Hume was well aware that we obtain a large number of our beliefs (which *we* are apt to call knowledge) from our conversational and literary commerce with other human beings, and he is widely held to have developed a certain kind of so-called "reductivist" theory of testimony, which purports to explain how this happens: *reductivist* because, so it is said, he treats testimony as if it were just a special case of inductive evidence. That theory, whether or not Hume is rightly credited with it, has become a focus of controversy in recent years and the debate about it raises some very central issues. In Chapter 6, I develop my own radical proposal: thinking about how testimony works as a source of beliefs, in my view, actually gives us a handle on the very idea of knowledge itself. Finally, in Chapter 7, we return to an issue, first raised by Plato and highlighted in Chapter 1: what is it about knowledge that makes us value it more highly than true beliefs? I believe that the theory developed in Chapter 6 provides a better answer to this fundamental question than other contemporary theories about the nature of knowledge.

I have avoided footnotes in the interest of maintaining the narrative flow. Indispensable references are incorporated into the text. I have, however, added a guide to further reading, which is intended to point readers to some of the relevant background to each chapter, as it occurs, and to advise those who want to pursue their interest in these topics more deeply.

Some of the ideas I present here have surfaced, at least in embryonic form, in some of my earlier writings. "Knowledge and enquiry", in Chapter 1 (pp. 9ff.), has its origins in "Meno's Paradox" (1986a). "The *Theaetetus* account", in Chapter 2 (pp. 27ff.), owes something to "What is knowledge? The structure of the argument in Plato's *Theaetetus*" (1987). A very distant ancestor of Chapter 5 is a paper I gave to the 21st Hume Conference, held at La Sapienza, Rome, in 1994, for which I received valuable support from the British Academy and the University of Bristol Arts Research Fund. I first began to explore the set of ideas presented in Chapter 6 in "The Transmission of Knowledge" (1979). They were further developed in *The Community of Knowledge* (1986b), published in the Scots Philosophical Monograph series by Aberdeen University Press, and reissued in Gregg Revivals by Ashgate Publishing Ltd in 1993. The theory contained in this book, however, is new. "The grammar of knowing and telling", Chapter 6 (pp. 115ff.), traces back to "A puzzle about telling" (1989). I am grateful to all the editors and publishers for permission to plunder these sources. I am also grateful to the Peters Fraser & Dunlop Group Ltd, acting for the Estate of Hilaire Belloc, for permission to quote the lines that appear on p. 75. The final shape of the book owes much to the very helpful comments of two anonymous readers for Acumen and the editor of the series in which it appears. Finally, I am grateful to my wife, Jill, for her forbearance while the book was being written and especially for her acute and sympathetic help in reading the penultimate version.

1 Beginning with Plato

Preamble

Plato was the first philosopher in the Western world to think seriously about the nature of knowledge. To him we owe most, if not all, of our basic philosophical questions on the subject, and he invented one way of addressing the issues which, in the past half century or so, after many hundreds of years, has come to dominate the field. I am going to use him in this chapter to introduce some important themes.

Plato's interest in knowledge is twofold. First, it is, for him, one among many proper topics for philosophical enquiry. It is something that human beings value, alongside justice, love, virtue, and beauty, to name a few other subjects of his investigations; because we think these things are valuable, it is natural that anyone of philosophical bent should want to understand clearly what they are. If we want people to act justly, for example, as we surely do, we need to know what just action involves. Similarly, if we want to obtain knowledge, it behoves us to get clear about what it is we want to obtain. But, secondly, as Plato conceives of it, knowledge is bound to be of special interest to anyone engaged in any philosophical enquiry at all, because knowledge, in a sense, is the object of all of them. Take the *Republic*. It is about justice. Plato embarks on this investigation because it is in our interest to learn what justice entails, to get to *know* what it is and to understand why it is worth pursuing. *Knowledge* is the whole point of the exercise: knowledge of what justice really is. For Plato this means understanding the nature of justice and hence what makes it valuable to us; for him there is an intimate connection between knowledge and understanding. Now, what goes for justice goes for anything else which might be a proper object of philosophical enquiry. We enquire into the nature of virtue or beauty or love because it is in our interest to get to *know* what they are so that we can cultivate them effectively. It follows that a philosopher who hasn't thought about knowledge cannot have thought about her own activity as a philosopher, no matter what specific enquiry she is pursuing; if she hasn't worked out what knowledge is, she can have no clear idea of what she is up to, what she is aiming at.

If we can get to know what justice is, so the thought runs, we shall be equipped to conduct ourselves justly, and consequently (as Plato believes) live a more genuinely satisfactory life. On the other hand, if we are ignorant about justice, we won't know how to behave in order to obtain the best quality of life for ourselves. In fact, Plato's mentor, Socrates, went further than this. Socrates held that knowledge of justice would inevitably translate into just conduct: no one, *knowing* what it is right or just to do, would ever do the opposite. And even if it is allowed, against Socrates, that people may sometimes act in ways which are contrary to what they know to be right, it will still be the case that getting to know what justice is has important practical implications for us. The *Republic*, perhaps the most ambitious and certainly the most famous of Plato's works, is primarily an investigation into the nature of justice; but in the light of the beliefs just mentioned it is fitting that a substantial part of the book should also be devoted to a discussion of knowledge. The *Republic* contains one of the three major Platonic discussions about knowledge on which I shall be drawing in this and the following chapter. The first may be found in a relatively early work, the *Meno*, and the third in a more mature work, the *Theaetetus,* generally thought to have been written somewhat later than the *Republic*. Plato's philosophy of knowledge is not easy. For one thing, it would be astonishing if there were no signs of development in his various works, written over several years. But it is hard to be sure whether what we find in these three books are different stages in the progressive development of a single unitary position, or, alternatively, whether he radically changed his views over time. What is definite is that he addresses the question "What is knowledge?" in different ways in these works and appears to offer different answers (or, as it turns out in the case of the *Theaetetus*, no answer at all).

High and low conceptions of knowledge

Plato's most fully elaborated theory about the nature of knowledge is the one in the *Republic*, where it is intimately linked to his celebrated theory of Forms. According to this theory, what a successful philosopher achieves, through painstaking intellectual enquiry, is knowledge of Forms: for example, knowledge of what Justice itself (the Form of Justice) is; or what Virtue itself or Beauty itself is. The Forms are, as it were, real but abstract essences which ideally can be apprehended by the intellect or understanding but are utterly inaccessible to the senses. Moreover, according to Plato's theory in the *Republic*, they are the only possible objects of *knowledge*. Unlike sense-objects they are eternal and unchanging. Sense-objects, by contrast, are in constant flux: for example, visible hues vary as the light varies, the sound of the car changes as it whizzes past us and so on. In Plato's eyes this disqualifies all things visible, audible or, more generally, sensible as objects of knowledge. Our senses license statements about how things *seem* to be to each of us at this moment or that, but they can never license statements about how things *really* are. Their domain is that of mere seeming, mere opinion, not knowledge.

The perpetually changing objects of sense-perception may imperfectly mimic the Forms, so it may not be altogether wrong to describe the building we see as, say, beautiful. But, Plato tells us, it cannot be perfectly (or *really*) beautiful; only Beauty itself, the unchanging Form, is *really* beautiful. What is really beautiful never changes and its beauty is pure, uncontaminated with other properties. The building, on the other hand, has many different properties jumbled together; at any moment it appears to have a certain shape and a certain colour or array of colours, and sometimes, perhaps, certain sounds and smells issue from it and sometimes they don't. This jumble of properties keeps changing over time, like everything else that we apprehend through the senses, and, in any case, all sense-objects decay as time progresses; none of them is everlasting. For our part, we are only able to describe a building as beautiful to the extent that we have at least an inkling of what is involved in being beautiful. That is, we have perhaps some faint and insecure understanding of the eternal and unchanging Form of Beauty and it is this Form that provides us with the standard by which beauty is to be measured. The mission of philosophy is to improve our understanding of the Forms, to secure our knowledge of them. The true philosopher, for Plato, is one who has accomplished this mission. The true philosopher, if there is one, will know perfectly, completely, what Beauty is (or Justice, or Love, or Knowledge, and so on).

According to the theory of knowledge that is correlative with the theory of Forms, knowledge is a state of an individual in virtue of which she has infallible, unerring insight into eternal truths through her intellectual grasp of the Forms. Her apprehension is such that it could not conceivably be mistaken. Plato was, perhaps, the first to elaborate a theory about the nature of knowledge of this extremely elevated kind; but others, too, have held similarly exalted views, although without his theory of Forms. According to Descartes, for example, in the second of his *Rules for the Direction of the Mind*, knowledge is certain and evident cognition, and we should resolve to believe only what is perfectly known and *incapable of being doubted*. Reason, underwritten by God, is able to engender this certain and evident cognition. When two people cannot agree, Descartes tells us, we can be sure that neither of them has knowledge, "for if the reasoning of one of them were certain and evident, he would be able to lay it before the other in such a way as eventually to convince his intellect as well". On this view we are *all*, to the extent that we are rational beings, capable of attaining knowledge of whatever truths are humanly attainable. These truths must be accessible to reason, so it is hardly surprising that mathematics should have become the paradigm of what can be known. The notion that what is known must be rationally demonstrable in the manner of mathematics is, on a long historical view, perhaps the prevailing thought about knowledge. It is nonetheless seriously at odds with our vernacular use of the vocabulary of knowledge, according to which it is perfectly possible for me to know now that it is raining since I can see that it is, and even perhaps for you to know now that it is raining when I tell you that it is.

Contemporary philosophers are apt to dismiss these elevated theories out of hand. The idea that knowledge might be self-authenticating, that our minds might apprehend truth in a manner which guarantees there is no error, is alien to our modern self-understanding. So it is not unusual for the distinguished proponents of such theories to be charged with error – even rather elementary error. In particular, they have sometimes been accused of misunderstanding an important truism: *if you know, you can't be wrong*. The suggestion is that they misinterpret this as saying that if you know something, the something you know is the sort of thing (like a truth of mathematics) which *could* not be otherwise than it is, so that you *could* not be mistaken if you believe it. But all the truism really says is: *if* you know that P, then (necessarily) it is the case that P. As far as this goes, P might be a simple empirical proposition like "it's raining". If I *know* it's raining, then it *is* raining. But it might not be raining; the truth could be otherwise. If it were, I could not *know* that it is raining, even though I might mistakenly believe that it is. Again, the truism does not say that if you know that P, then your state of mind is such as to be able to filter out error, an infallible truth-attaining state. *All* that is said is that if it is not the case that P, then it cannot be correct to describe your state as one of knowing that P. But Plato and Descartes (and others), who did believe that human beings were capable of a state that infallibly accessed truth, should not be lightly charged with mistaking the import of a rather elementary point about the *logic* of knowledge. The suggestion that they did gets things the wrong way round. The fact is, I think, that they each of them had a particular vision of what a human being is. According to their vision, we are essentially rational and immortal beings, temporarily encumbered with bodies, and liable to be confused by our very imperfect information-gathering faculties – the senses. It is because this is our essential nature that truth is, so to speak, our birthright; it can be attained with certainty when our rational nature is given free play, unmuddied by the senses, and *knowledge* is the name we give to our state when we have actually accessed it. What we will have accessed, on this view, can only be the sort of thing (like a mathematical truth) that is accessible to reason.

This vision of what human beings are has an important place in the history of our culture and it deserves our respect even if it we don't share it. A philosopher who thinks in this way about our essential nature will find that the concept of knowledge, having the logical property encapsulated in our truism, is apt for expressing our apprehension of eternal and unchanging truths: the truths of mathematics, for example. It would be dangerous and wrong, however, to treat the fact that we possess this concept as a premise for a knockdown argument in favour of this kind of theory about our real nature and the real nature of the things we can know about; at one key point in the *Republic*, Plato certainly does use our possession of the concept as tending to confirm his theory (*Republic* 476d–480a), but he only presents it as a suggestive line of thought that might help to persuade a Form-sceptic of the truth of the theory.

We, for our part, should certainly be interested in the fact that we operate with a concept that has this property, namely, that if you know, you can't be wrong. It is one of a number of properties that any theory about knowledge needs somehow to accommodate and explain. One might perhaps view the elevated theories about human nature and its cognitive powers to be found in writers like Plato and Descartes as attempts to rationalize our possession of such a concept. But the fact is, of course, that we are all liable to make mistakes; we *are* rational beings, but, alas, we are not purely rational and we may become confused by the contingencies of our material existence. A lot of the philosophy of knowledge may be construed as an attempt to reach an accommodation with this human liability to err.

We return now to Plato. He himself, in later works, came to see that there were difficulties in the theory of Forms and hence in the correlative theory of knowledge. Indeed the Forms are not even mentioned in the *Theaetetus*. We may ask, does this silence reflect Plato's disenchantment with the theory when he came to write this dialogue? Or are the Forms meant to be conspicuous through their absence from a dialogue which, failing to deliver a positive account of knowledge, leaves us only with the somewhat less than cheering consolation that at least we now know that we don't know what knowledge is? Is the moral meant to be, as some have thought, that a satisfactory account of what knowledge is cannot be given without reference to these supposed objects of knowledge? Or has Plato abandoned that theory?

This is not the place to try to resolve such interpretative issues. What we do need to notice, however, is this: Plato, notwithstanding the exalted doctrine of the *Republic*, for which he is most renowned, often seems to be friendly to an apparently less lofty, more workaday conception of knowledge. At all events, he seems to be happy in other works to use much less exalted instances of knowledge in order to illustrate key features of the concept on which he wishes to insist.

These key features include the notions of expertise and teaching on which the *Republic* itself puts great emphasis. The philosopher-kings of the state which Plato describes combine sovereign political authority with the epistemic authority that comes from knowledge of the Forms. They are expert on such matters as justice and right living. They have the authority, both epistemic and political, to tell others how to live. And those of us who are not expert but recognize that it is in our interest to live just lives can only defer to them. (Those who do not recognize where their best interests lie should, according to Plato, be made to conform (*Republic*: 590c–d).) Moreover, the knowledge that these experts possess can be taught, but not to everybody. The *Republic* painstakingly outlines the curriculum which should be used to engender knowledge of the Forms, but only very few people actually have the intellectual capacity to pursue it. Still, that the knowledge can be taught is an important feature of the scenario which the *Republic* develops. It means that the state has a future; provided a proper programme of education is put into place, future generations can acquire the expertise that is necessary to provide the only sort of government which can ensure that the state will flourish. (But in the long run, so Plato thinks, no state subsisting in the material world can flourish for ever. Corruption and decay are ultimately inevitable, although their onset may be delayed by the actions of knowledgeable rulers. One of the most important elements in the *Republic* is Plato's mapping of the supposedly inevitable steps in the process of decay.)

Plato's linking of the concept of knowledge with the ideas of teaching and of expertise seems intuitively right. So perhaps this is another feature of the concept, to put alongside our truism (*if you know, you can't be wrong*), which any theory about knowledge needs to accommodate and explain. It is not peculiar to lofty theories, like that of the *Republic*. In fact, in both the *Meno* and the *Theaetetus*, we find that Plato illustrates this aspect of knowledge with lowly examples. In the *Meno*, we are told that *anything* that counts as knowledge may be taught, and anything that may be taught counts as knowledge. The underlying thought is that a master, in command of a branch of knowledge, can teach it to his apprentices. In the *Theaetetus*, this notion of expert knowledge, evidently thought to be utterly familiar, is enlisted to make a very important and substantive point against relativism, a type of theory that Plato utterly abhors; we shall discuss this later. What matters here is that the point is illustrated with a range of mostly mundane examples of expertise: medicine, wine-growing, gymnastics, music and cookery (*Theaetetus* 178b ff.).

Perhaps the lesson to be drawn is this. Even if at the end of the day we resolved, with Plato of the *Republic*, that what cobblers and cooks have is unworthy to be called knowledge on account of the impermanent, shifting nature of the material matters they "know" about, we might nevertheless learn something about what we understand by knowledge from observing the implications that attributions of knowledge have, even in these common or garden cases. We might think it wrong to include these humdrum arts and crafts in the *extension* of the concept – those items to which it is correctly applied – but our workaday thinking about them may nevertheless be a reflection of our innate understanding of its *intension* – the sense it carries.

This, at any rate, would be a way of reconciling what on the face of it are radically inconsistent positions in Plato's *œuvre*: on the one hand, the high view of the *Republic*, according to which the only possible objects of knowledge are Forms, which knowledge may only be won through rigorous intellectual effort; and on the other hand, the fact that in other dialogues he frequently includes as examples of knowledge anything that a master might teach to his apprentices. But, of course, it might be that in the *Meno*, Plato had not yet worked out the lofty view he was to present in the *Republic*, and that in the *Theaetetus* he was already inclined to renounce it. Finally, we may note that there is one place in the *Theaetetus* where he apparently commits himself to saying that only an *eyewitness* could know what happened on some particular occasion (*Theaetetus* 201b–c); the position advanced in the *Republic* is that whatever *eyewitnessing* supplies, it cannot possibly be *knowledge*, because nothing obtained through the senses could ever count as knowledge.

There is one last point worth mentioning in connection with these examples. We apply the concept of knowledge in two ways. We use it to refer to the state of an individual who knows, say, this or that theorem in geometry or the principles of the internal combustion engine, but we also use it to refer to those branches of knowledge we call geometry or automotive engineering, branches of knowledge that can be taught to students and apprentices. This second application is marked in Greek by the availability of a plural in the standard word for knowledge. In the *Theaetetus*, Plato speaks of "knowledges" as easily as we speak of sciences. We need to keep in mind that the application we favour most may make a difference to our account of knowledge.

In the remainder of this chapter we shall examine two seminal moments from the first of the Platonic works mentioned, the *Meno*.

Knowledge and enquiry

As we have seen, knowledge is the object of all philosophical enquiries; it is also the typical object of any enquiry whatsoever. If you want to know the time, as we say, ask a policeman. The school teacher who asks her class who the first President of the USA was does not perhaps want to know the answer to this question, since she may know it already; but she certainly wants to know something – whether her pupils know the answer. So, quite generally, the object of enquiry is knowledge. But it may seem there is a paradox here. At all events, the *Meno* starts its serious discussion of the subject with a puzzle about this, a puzzle sometimes called "Meno's Paradox".

At first this may come across as an irritating and rather trivial riddle, but in fact it has real substance. It arises as follows. Meno asks Socrates the question around which the dialogue is officially framed: can virtue (good behaviour, perhaps) be taught or is it something innate or, again, is it something that only comes with practice, like a skill? By way of response, Socrates adopts a characteristic posture: he says he is in no position to answer questions *about* virtue because he doesn't know at all what virtue is. This is typical; Socrates standardly claims to be completely ignorant about the subjects of the dialogues in which he is protagonist. Meno, on the other hand, is presented, from the beginning, as a know-all, the kind of brash individual who is prepared to answer questions about anything at all (*Meno* 70b–c), so he is happy to tell Socrates what virtue is. The contrast between the two is deliberate. In fact, it soon transpires that Meno is not as knowledgeable as he thought he was. At all events, it doesn't take Socrates long to demonstrate the inadequacy of his attempts to answer the question on which Socrates is stalled. As Plato sets it up, Socrates, with a little deft interrogation, not only shows the deficiencies of the various answers that Meno tries out, but actually succeeds in persuading Meno himself that they are deficient. Meno, for his part, confesses to complete bewilderment; it is, we are told, as if he had been numbed by a stingray. Socrates, it seems, has a kind of magic capacity to induce confusion in his interlocutors (*Meno* 80a–b). At this point, Socrates proposes that he and Meno together undertake a joint enquiry into the nature of virtue. This is what prompts Meno to present his puzzle. How, Meno asks, can Socrates engage in this enquiry if he really is, as he claims, *completely* ignorant about what virtue is? Meno thinks his own position is different. Although he has been muddled by Socrates, he still thinks he really does know the answer to the question; merely, in his confusion he can't at present get the answer straight – a condition with which, I daresay, many people will be familiar. But, given time to recover his equilibrium, there is no reason to think, so he suggests, that he couldn't answer the question; really (deep down), he does know what virtue is. Socrates, however, being completely ignorant, is in a quite different plight. Here is Meno's puzzle:

> A man cannot try to discover either what he knows or what he does not know. He would not seek what he knows, for since he knows it there is no need of the enquiry, nor what he does not know, for in that case he does not even know what he is to look for. (*Meno* 80e)

In other words, if at the outset you already know what you want to know, you have no need to make an enquiry; and if you don't know what you want to know, you can't even get an enquiry off the ground. Any enquiry is going to be either disingenuous (you know the answer already) or impossible (you don't even know what you're after, so the enquiry is, as it were, objectless).

Of course, this is nonsense (as Plato knew perfectly well). But it forces us to consider what the requirements of genuine enquiry are. Enquiries can take many forms. Indeed, not every serious enquiry can be framed at the outset as a quest for some definite bit of knowledge. The starting point of a lot of philosophy, and very likely of some science, too, is something much vaguer: an unease or perplexity that demands attention; a hunch that needs articulating and exploring; an itch that needs scratching. These more vaguely focused enquiries, however, are liable to throw up more definite questions as they proceed, and enquiries that do seek definite bits of knowledge are, surely, the most basic. You ask the man in the street if he knows the way to the railway station in the hope that he can provide you with the information you are seeking; or you wonder to yourself whether the post has arrived and go and look in your letter box to find out. Meno's puzzle is about these most basic information-seeking enquiries. One way of seeing it is as a sort of verbal sleight of hand designed to distract our attention from what is really obvious. For the truth is that, in a certain sense, any enquirer of this elementary sort *does* know what she wants to know and currently doesn't know. She is perfectly well able to identify her ignorance both to herself and to other people. She does it by means of the interrogative expression she uses to frame her question. Thus, the utterance "Where's the key?", on some occasion of its serious use, identifies an ignorance of the speaker and its utterance constitutes a request that that very ignorance be remedied. The cure for ignorance is knowledge; the speaker wants to know where the key is and hopes her interlocutor can supply the knowledge she wants. Our interrogative words – *who*, *what*, *where*, *when* and so on – enable us to identify bits of information, bits of knowledge, even when we cannot spell them out. It is impossible to exaggerate the importance of this humble linguistic device. If we didn't have it, enquiry would be impossible. The most obvious constraint on enquiry is that we be able to identify what we want to know, that we *do* know (in this sense) what we want to know. And even the vaguer enquiries mentioned just now must, surely, get a sharper focus in time. Happily, and it is a very important fact about human beings – easily overlooked but vital for our very mode of being – we have the means of identifying what we want to know and do not know, of identifying our ignorances quite precisely. It is what interrogative constructions fundamentally are for. Socrates, notwithstanding his professed total ignorance on the subject, knows perfectly well what he wants to know; he wants to know *what virtue is*. At one level, Meno's Paradox works by distracting our attention from the existence and use of interrogative words, by means of which we are able to identify bits of knowledge without spelling them out.

There is much more to the puzzle than this, however. Early on, as we have seen, Meno professes to know what virtue is. There is a suggestion that he may have learnt the answer from a noted expert, Gorgias, and he is amazed that Socrates, on his own telling, doesn't know at all what it is; there are plenty of experts around whom he could ask and anyway it is surprising that Socrates, given his reputation, isn't one of them. Being (in his own estimation) an expert, Meno thinks he is in a position to enlighten Socrates, to *tell* him the answer to the question "What is virtue?", and Socrates invites him to do so (*Meno* 71c). It is only when this self-styled expert fails to come up with an answer which can withstand Socratic scrutiny that Socrates proposes they cooperate in an enquiry. This will involve a different mode of enquiry, however. The first kind we might call *market-place enquiry*, enquiry of other people. When you seek information from another person, you cast them in the role of expert. You want to know where the railway station is, and you ask the stranger in the street, in the hope that they have the expert local knowledge that you lack; or Socrates, disingenuously no doubt, wanting to know what virtue is, asks Meno, the self-styled "expert", to tell him.

When market-place enquiry predictably fails to deliver an acceptable answer to Socrates' question, it seems he is compelled to enquire in a different mode, which I shall call *Cartesian enquiry*, after Descartes, its most renowned exponent. Descartes's philosophy is founded on mistrust of so-called experts or authorities, and the Cartesian enquirer does not ask another person to supply the information she wants, but looks for it on her own. The name sounds rather grand, but Cartesian enquiries are often pretty mundane; when I go to see if the post has arrived I am, in effect, enquiring in the Cartesian mode. Now what Socrates proposes to Meno is that they cooperate in a Cartesian enquiry. Meno is to abandon the role of expert about virtue and adopt instead the role of a humble seeker after truth on the same level as Socrates. They will work together to try to sort out for themselves what virtue is, but they will not enquire of other people. It is this proposal that triggers Meno's puzzle and gives it its teeth; it is evident from the high seriousness of the response it elicits that Plato took it very seriously indeed. It would, in any case, have been out of character for Plato's Meno to raise a puzzle about market-place enquiry since, as a self-styled expert, he is committed to its validity; he must think those who ask him about matters on which he is expert can as a rule obtain what they lack and want.

How are we to understand Cartesian enquiries, the enquiries to which we are driven when there are no informed experts we can turn to? How do they work? One possible model is scrutiny: the Cartesian enquirer looks and sees for herself. "What happens", we may imagine the solitary scientist or the experimental cook asking herself, "if I mix this with that?" and they go ahead and do it in order to find out. They look and see. They scrutinize the world in order to discover its properties or whether it has some particular property. So, perhaps, the solitary philosopher asks herself if virtue is teachable, and she brings virtue, or rather the idea of virtue, into view in the privacy of her study; she mulls over the concept in order to determine, in the light of her examination, whether virtue is teachable or not. Historically, a good deal of philosophical enquiry has had this armchair character. The philosopher focuses on some concept with which she is more or less familiar and sets about the task of examining its properties and describing it in detail. But in order to enquire by scrutiny, the enquirer must somehow focus on the object whose properties or behaviour is to be investigated; it must be brought into view either *really*, in the kitchen, the laboratory or wherever, or *conceptually*, in the mind. And this method is manifestly not available to anyone in the position that Socrates adopts. He does not know *at all* what virtue is, so there can be no question of his scrutinizing it. He is in no position to examine the idea of virtue with his mind's eye, so to speak, so as to see whether it is teachable. Not knowing at all what virtue is, he is in no position to focus on it in order to scrutinize its properties.

A different model for Cartesian enquiry might be the model of searching. In fact, the Greek word for enquiry that Plato uses is also the standard Greek for seeking, looking for. This provides the model in terms of which Meno's puzzle is framed. The idea is that you can't search for something if you don't know what you are looking for, and you can't look for it exactly, if you've already got it clearly in view, before your very eyes.

It's the first leg that matters here. Consider this. There are, on a street in Bristol, some pedestal tables of bronze known as the Nails. In days gone by, merchants, transacting their business, paid their debts "on the nail", as we still say. The Nails are now a well-known tourist attraction, and we can easily imagine a tourist looking for them. Any guidebook will tell her about them. But imagine a tourist without a guidebook who has simply no idea at all what the Bristol Nails are. How could such a person possibly look for them? Even if she ran up against them, how could she know that they were what she was looking for? Socrates, being, as he professes, completely ignorant about virtue, would be like this tourist if we construe his enquiry as a search for something. In terms of this model there is just no escaping the quandary Meno presents him with.

The fundamental point is that you cannot search for X, whatever X may be, unless you are from the outset equipped with a good enough notion of what X is to provide you with criteria by which to judge whether you have found what you were looking for. You must have some idea of X if you are to look for it. But Socrates tells us he has no idea at all what virtue is. He is asking what virtue is from a position of *complete* ignorance. It follows that he is in no position to search for it. And the model of scrutiny won't work for him either: since he is completely ignorant, there is nothing he can focus his mind on. Thus it seems we must urgently consider whether there may not be some alternative way of construing the enquiry. This point is not merely of academic or historical interest – an issue for Plato and his interpreters. It is highly germane to the enquiry *we* are engaged on. Our interest is in the question "What is knowledge?" This is exactly the sort of (what is . . .?) question that Socrates is always asking; and, just like Socrates, we need to understand the grammar, as it were, of our question, if we are to have any idea how to set about answering it. Here notice the reflexive bearing of Plato's enquiry about knowledge on the very kind of enquiry he himself is engaged on. What goes for Plato goes for us.

It may be thought that the difficulty I have just described will also arise for someone engaged in market-place enquiry: for example, the tourist who asks someone in the Tourist Information Office, "What are the Nails, and where are they?" Just as we need criteria by which to judge whether our Cartesian search has been successful, so, it may be said, we need criteria by which to judge whether the answer a respondent gives us is true. But this rests on a misunderstanding. Even the Bristol tourist, guidebook in hand, could mistake some other bit of street furniture for the Nails. If she makes a mistake, this doesn't mean she doesn't have criteria by which to judge whether she has been successful. She needs criteria even to make a mistaken judgement. Only on this condition can she say with sincerity and conviction, "Here are the Nails, at last". The unguided tourist, who doesn't know at all what the Nails are, can have no criteria of success and is in no position even to make a *mistaken* judgement. The constraints on market-place enquiry are different. Here the enquirer must be able to recognize *an* answer to her question; this is a condition on her *having* a question in mind. But whether she should accept an answer she is given must be in the end, provided it is recognizably a possible answer, a matter of trust. She could not be forearmed with criteria by which to judge (even mistakenly) that she had been given the truth. Nevertheless, in the last analysis, there is, perhaps, no very deep difference between the two kinds of case. Both enquirers need sufficient understanding to recognize possible conclusions to their enquiry. The Cartesian seeker has criteria by which to judge (even mistakenly) that some object matches the specification of the object of her search. The market-place enquirer understands her question sufficiently well to recognize a possible answer which, rightly or wrongly, she may decide to accept or reject. Without that understanding she cannot have a real question in mind.

Now how does Socrates address Meno's puzzle? In effect, he dodges it by abandoning the position which prompted it. He presents us with a theory that denies after all that he is completely ignorant about the nature of virtue. The theory says that knowledge of things like virtue is actually innate; in terms suggested by the theory of Forms, still to be developed in the *Republic*, our rational souls are already acquainted with the Forms of Virtue, Justice, Love and so on when we are born. Socrates' plight is not really that he does not *know* what virtue is, rather he cannot now *recall* what it is; his mind is clouded and confused, although in reality at some deep level he does know. He is in exactly the same plight as Meno takes himself to be in after he has been bemused by Socrates' interrogation. The difference between them is that Meno was unduly confident of his ability to tell us what virtue is and came up with wrong ideas, which he mistook for knowledge. On Plato's theory, knowledge of such things lies pretty deep, and can only be elicited (recalled, as he says) by a disciplined rational investigation.

Before we leave this topic, we should note a point to which we shall have to return later. Throughout the discussion, the word *know* and its cognates have been harnessed in aid of understanding the nature of enquiry. And Meno's puzzle was framed in the vocabulary of *knowledge*. It could hardly be otherwise. In particular, it would be hard, if not impossible, to reframe the discussion in the vocabulary of belief, as the reader may verify by trying to substitute *believe* for *know* in its formulation. The vocabulary of belief is simply inapt in this context. And in fact the language provides us with a striking hint that there is a deep affinity between the idea of knowledge and that of enquiry. Socrates wants to know what virtue is. It would make no sense to say he wants to *believe* what virtue is. What could this mean? The verb *believe*, together with its confrères like *hold*, *think*, *maintain*, *opine* and so on, will not tolerate interrogative constructions after it; that is, it will not allow those constructions which enable a speaker to identify the facts to which they refer without describing them in articulate detail. Whatever the explanation of this grammatical fact, it means that the vocabulary of *knowledge* is apt for certain purposes for which the vocabulary of *belief* is not. And this we may add to our catalogue of features about knowledge which a theory of knowledge needs to accommodate and account for.

Meno's Challenge

Near the end of the dialogue that bears his name, Meno challenges Socrates to explain why knowledge should be esteemed as highly as it is and, in particular, why it should be esteemed more highly than *doxa*, variously translated as belief, opinion, and (in some contexts) judgement. The fundamental idea underlying *doxa* is that of the way things *seem* to be to someone, the way they take them to be. In what follows I shall use *belief* and *opinion*, together with their cognates and any other convenient synonym.

Here is Meno's Challenge:

> SOCRATES   Let me explain. If someone knows the way to Larissa, or anywhere else you like, then when he goes there and takes others with him he will be a good and capable guide, you would agree?
>
> MENO   Of course.
>
> SOCRATES   But if a man judges correctly which is the road, though he has never been there and doesn't know it, will he not also guide others aright?
>
> MENO   Yes he will.
>
> SOCRATES   And as long as he has a correct opinion on the points about which the other had knowledge, he will be just as good a guide, believing the truth but not knowing it.
>
> MENO   Just as good.
>
> SOCRATES   Therefore true opinion is as good a guide as knowledge for the purpose of acting rightly . . .
>
> MENO   Except that the man with knowledge will always be successful, and the man with right opinion only sometimes.
>
> SOCRATES   What? Will he not always be successful so long as he has the right opinion?
>
> MENO   That must be so, I suppose. In that case, *I wonder why knowledge should be so much more prized than right opinion, and indeed how there is any difference between them.*
>
> > (*Meno* 97a–d; emphasis added)

The thought is this. We can only fit our actions to our wishes in the light of our representations of how things are. We want and value states of mind that accurately represent how things are because (trivially) we want to achieve our goals; misrepresentations can lead to inappropriate actions, actions that don't promote our objectives and may even frustrate them. Suppose we want to go out, and the forecasters are right in predicting rain: in this instance, it is good if we think it is going to rain and bad if we think it isn't. In the former case, having a correct representation of how the weather will be, we may take an umbrella and so stay dry (supposing that that is what we want – we might *want* to get wet). In the latter case, because our representation is wrong, we risk getting wet by not taking an umbrella, when we would rather have stayed dry. Now a correct opinion is a correct representation of how things actually are (or were or will be), so surely for practical purposes this is the best representational state to be in. What more could we want? Moreover, if "knowledge" is our name for the best representational state of mind, it looks as if correct opinion *is* knowledge. At all events, if knowledge is not correct opinion, then we need to understand what the difference is and why knowledge should be prized more highly than correct opinion.

The question that Plato makes Meno raise here is the most fundamental in the philosophy of knowledge – a question against which any theory about knowledge needs to be tested. In fact Plato, in the person of Socrates, immediately hazards an answer of his own, although he carefully disclaims *knowing* that it is the correct answer. His answer is sketchy, metaphorical and hard to understand; and it isn't clear that he stuck with it in more mature works. One might read the material about knowledge and belief in the *Republic* as a later attempt to put flesh on these meagre metaphorical bones; but the *Republic* envisages a more radical difference between knowledge and belief than the *Meno* seems to allow.

Before we look more closely at Plato's response to this challenge, let us review in broad terms what the possibilities might be. It seems there are going to be two possible and incompatible types of approach, traces of both of which can be discovered in Plato's writings. One approach would represent knowing as a state of a person which is of a totally different kind from believing or opining. This has been called the "generic difference response" to the Challenge. The high conception of knowledge found in the *Republic* is an example. According to this conception, knowledge is intrinsically more valuable because it accesses reality, it is necessarily truth attaining, and the person with knowledge is apprised of truths of the most important kind, which it behoves us to know (cf. *Republic* 504d ff.). Beliefs, by contrast, are locked into the world of the senses, the domain of mere appearances. So knowledge and belief are utterly different in kind. This conception of knowledge takes us a long way from the context in which Meno's Challenge was mounted – finding the right route for Larissa – but then Plato's position might be that with mundane matters like getting from Athens to Larissa there really is nothing more useful than true opinion, and, indeed, that nothing better than true opinion is available in such cases. Knowledge is necessary for a correct understanding of mathematics and other high sciences, and also of the values that ideally should inform our lives. These, on the high conception, are the proper objects of knowledge. But they have no impact on such matters as the route to Larissa, about which only opinion is possible. In opposition to this, some commentators seem to think Plato believes that first-hand experience of the route is superior to (mere) true opinion and will count as knowledge; I think this reads more into the text than it supports. But if Plato had thought this he would have been wrong. I have driven to Nempnett Thrubwell, but if I wanted to drive there again, I would do better to rely on a decent map than on my recollection of the route.

This is not the only form that a generic difference response may take. It could be the case, and in due course I shall argue that it is the case, that we value knowledge highly because of the special role which the concept plays in the conduct of our lives. There is no difference in kind between the sorts of things one can know about and the sorts of things about which one has beliefs. In particular, no matter how lowly some item of belief might be, it could also be represented properly, in certain circumstances, as an item of knowledge; and no matter how grand an item of knowledge might be, it could also be represented properly, in appropriate circumstances, as an item of belief. What matters is the commitments and the implications of these different styles of representations.

A different kind of response to Meno's Challenge will concede that knowing entails believing. On this view, the difference between knowledge and belief consists in the fact that although someone who knows that P believes that P and is correct in so doing, the belief must, additionally, have a special feature that elevates it to the level of knowledge. This has been called the "differentiating component response". Plato's own immediate response in the *Meno* is of this sort. It generates what, in recent times, has become far and away the commonest way of trying to explain the concept of knowledge: the so-called "tripartite analysis", already mentioned in the Introduction. This has it that if A knows that P, then:

1. A believes that P
2. A's belief that P is true
3. A's belief is . . .

Again, we need to be aware that there can be quite radical differences in the way the differentiating component is conceived and the third clause of the analysis completed. In Chapter 3 we shall examine some modern theories that follow this pattern. In doing so, we need to bear in mind that Meno challenges us not only to say what the difference is between knowledge and true belief but also to account for the fact that knowledge is valued more highly. We need to weigh the credentials of proposed completions of the third clause in the light of this aspect of the Challenge.

There are several ways in which the differentiating component response might be developed. First, it may be suggested that what makes the difference between knowing and believing is the individual's *understanding*. Thus, in his *Essay Concerning Human Understanding*, John Locke (1632–1704) remarked:

> So much as we ourselves consider and comprehend of truth and reason, so much we possess of real and true knowledge. The floating of other men's opinions in our brains makes us not one jot the more knowing, though they happen to be true.
> (1975: 1, 4, 23)

This is, in fact, quite Platonic. In both the *Meno* and the *Theaetetus*, Plato may be construed as suggesting that true beliefs may amount to knowledge if they have a proper component of understanding. In the *Republic* the position is more radical: understanding is not only a necessary aspect of knowledge, but it is also necessarily absent from belief.

In modern times, the differentiating component has more often been thought to consist in something like *justification*. Roughly speaking, the idea is that A's belief amounts to knowledge if in addition to the belief's being true A is justified in holding it, holds it for good reasons, with adequate evidence and so on. It is important not to confuse these two positions. According to the second (justificationist) view, someone might justifiably believe and thus know that the square on the hypotenuse of a right-angled triangle is equal to the sum of the squares on the other two sides (Pythagoras' theorem), but not be able to follow the proof, let alone prove it for themselves. Their justification for believing it might, nonetheless, be adequate. They have read it in a reliable textbook, or they recall it from their schooldays and recall that it was provable, or even remember that they were once able to prove it themselves, and so on. According to the first position, however, no one of whom this was true would know the theorem because their understanding would be defective.

In 1963, Edmund Gettier published a famous article in which he exposed serious difficulties in the idea that true belief with justification might amount to knowledge (Gettier 1963). In subsequent years, a vast amount of work in the philosophy of knowledge has been devoted to the task of finding an analysis of knowledge in terms of belief which is immune to Gettier's argument. This has often taken the form of attempts to elaborate the justificationist account. But some, despairing of that approach, have tried yet another tack. On this, the third form of tripartite analysis, A knows that P when her true belief that P is properly connected to the state of affairs she believes to obtain. The simplest and original version takes the connection to be straightforwardly causal. You know that P when your believing that P is caused by the fact that P. Theories of this genre are often referred to as "externalist" since they require a connection between the believer's state of mind and facts external to her mind which she believes to obtain. Or perhaps we should say, since the facts one believes to obtain may be and sometimes are facts internal to oneself, that these theories require a connection between her state of mind and what she believes that, like a causal connection, is of a kind that could hold between her mind and external states of affairs. In contrast with this, theories that require that the believer be justified in holding what she does, that she should have weighed the evidence adequately and so on, are often called "internalist". What makes the difference is something internal to the subject. In fact, of course, there is always going to be one externalist component in any analysis: the requirement that the belief be true.

In this chapter we have used Plato to set the scene. As we have proceeded we have noted various features about our concept of knowledge that a good theory needs to accommodate and account for. In particular, we noted the logical point informally put by saying "if you know, you can't be wrong" (p. 6). We noted that the concept of knowledge seems to support notions of expertise, authority and the possibility of teaching (p. 7), all recognized by Plato. In this connection we also noted that the concept is used sometimes to refer to the state of an individual knower and sometimes to what she knows and what can be taught to others (p. 7). Finally, we drew attention to the apparent affinity between knowledge and enquiry enshrined in the grammar of our language, in the fact that *know* takes the interrogative constructions we standardly use to frame enquiries and identify ignorances, while *believe* and its confrères do not (p. 16). In Chapter 2 we shall look in more detail at Plato's responses to Meno's Challenge.

Analysing knowledge
2 Plato's way

The *Meno* account

As we have already noted, Plato's own response to Meno's Challenge in the dialogue that bears his name is metaphorical and thin, and it is hard to know what to make of it. It is, however, the first gesture we have in the direction of a tripartite analysis. Socrates puts it forward in the light of the recollection theory that he has just presented as his response to Meno's Paradox. The idea, it will be remembered, is this: when we ask questions such as "What is knowledge?", "What is virtue?", and so on, there is a sense in which we *do* know the answers already, having learnt them in some previous mode of existence; merely we do not remember them very clearly.

Plato illustrates this idea dramatically. He makes Socrates summon an uneducated slave and confront him with a question in geometry. First, Socrates draws a square whose sides are two feet by two feet. The slave sees at once that the area of the square is four square feet. The question is, if we double the area, making it eight square feet, how long will the sides then be? The slave immediately replies that they will be double, that is, each will be four feet. In fact, of course, this instant, intuitive answer is wrong. Plato now has Socrates subject the slave to a series of questions; it is an essential element of this little drama that at no point does Socrates actually *tell* the slave anything to the point. Nevertheless, there comes a stage where the slave appreciates that his first answer was wrong, at which juncture Socrates delivers the following commentary:

> Observe, Meno, the stage he has reached on the path of recollection. At the beginning he did not know the side of the square of eight feet. Nor indeed does he know it now, but then he thought he knew it and answered boldly, as was appropriate – he felt no perplexity. Now, however, he does feel perplexed. Not only does he not know the answer; he does not even think he knows it. . . . Isn't he in a better position now in relation to what he didn't know? . . . In perplexing him and numbing him like the stingray, have we done him any harm? (*Meno* 84a–b)

This mention of the numbing effect of Socrates' interrogation is, of course, a reference to the condition Meno found himself in earlier in the dialogue, when, having delivered his over-confident account of the nature of virtue, he found himself bemused by Socrates. Eventually, after further questioning but still no telling, the slave comes up with the correct answer that the side of the doubled square will be the same as the diagonal of the original square. And then we get some more commentary:

> SOCRATES   But these opinions (the correct ones) were some-where in him, were they not?
> MENO   Yes. [They had to be: Socrates supposedly had *told* him nothing.]
> SOCRATES   So a man who does not know has in himself true opinions on a subject without having knowledge.
> MENO   It would appear so.
> SOCRATES   At present those opinions, being newly aroused, have a dream-like quality. But if the same questions are put to him on many occasions and in different ways, you can see that in the end he will have a knowledge on the subject as accurate as anybody's. (*Meno* 85c)

So how does Plato answer Meno's Challenge? He tells us, through the person of Socrates, that mere opinions, mere beliefs, even when they are true, are unstable; they are like the legendary automata crafted by Daedalus, they are apt to "run away" from a man's mind. They are not worth much until they have been tethered, fastened down by "working out the reason" (*aitias logismos*) (*Meno* 98a). The little drama with the slave illustrates this process. The tether,

Plato tells us, is what makes the difference between knowledge and right opinion, and it is what makes knowledge more valuable than mere right opinion. The steps in the process seem to be as follows. First, the slave's memory of the truth is awakened by means of a critical interrogation of his first faulty response. At this point he has an opinion that is true. Then his grasp of the truth is made secure by reiterating the steps that aroused his memory in the first place and by presenting fresh arguments to the same conclusion. So he ends up with knowledge that formerly he thought he did not possess.

There is some lack of clarity in this account. Plato's solution to Meno's Paradox involved the idea that really we already know the answers to the questions whose answers we seek. But when the questions are first put to the slave, it seems that the knowledge-making tether has not yet been fashioned; and Socrates himself says that at this point he only has true opinions in him. So how can it be said that he knows at that point? Perhaps the idea is that at the beginning of an enquiry we have (temporarily) forgotten *both* the truth *and* its rationale. There are two aspects to knowledge: an apprehension of the truth and the understanding that secures that apprehension. Both need to be reawakened, but typically we can be brought, like the slave, to the point of assenting to the truth before we have perfectly recovered our understanding of the rationale.

Let us remind ourselves of the essential steps in the process; it is the prototype of a style of philosophical enquiry that, as we shall see, survives to this day. An answer to a question is hazarded and put to the test by Socratic questioning; it is found to be incorrect in the light of the intuitions that this questioning awakens. So that answer is reformed or a completely new answer is proposed and this, too, is tested in its turn. And so on, until finally the true answer is found, the latent knowledge exposed and secured. In the *Theaetetus*, to which we shall turn shortly, Plato brings a famous metaphor to bear on this process. Here he makes Socrates describe himself as a midwife of other people's ideas (*Theaetetus* 148e–151d). His role as midwife is to test his interlocutors' first off-the-cuff answers to "What is X?" questions, causing them both to appreciate the deficiencies of these answers and to suggest improvements by calling on their own inner resources of latent knowledge. At the end of the enquiry, either a viable answer will have been brought to birth or it will have been found that the interlocutors' initial answers were only signs of a phantom pregnancy.

In the *Meno*, curiously, the account of knowledge, produced in response to Meno's Challenge, is not itself subjected to this classic treatment, for which the *Meno* is supposed to provide a theoretical foundation. The *Theaetetus*, however, more mature and more advanced than the *Meno*, may perhaps be viewed as providing what the *Meno* lacks. Unfortunately, there is no live birth at the end.

Before we come to that, there are two matters to discuss concerning the *Meno* account. First, why should working out the *aitias logismos* tether a belief, make it stable and secure, prevent its running away? Take what in our eyes will surely be the most favourable kind of case for Plato, the proof of a theorem in mathematics. The mathematician has worked out the proof that establishes the conjecture, C, from which she started; she now believes C with complete confidence and she has the proof at her command. Moreover, it is, let us grant, a valid proof from true premises. It does not follow that our mathematician cannot be dislodged from her belief in C. We may sap her confidence by reminding her of the past occasions when she has been convinced by bogus "proofs"; despite her cleverness at proving things, she is, perhaps, constitutionally diffident and thus easy to undermine. Alternatively, we can imagine someone of stubborn disposition being convinced of the truth of some (true) proposition by a bad proof they have excogitated; such a person might only be confirmed in her error by the *aitias logismos* she believed herself to have found. The fact is that Plato's claim about the powers of an *aitias logismos* to tether true beliefs seems to be of dubious psychological validity, if this means making them permanently available to the subject in the way that my belief that I live in Bristol is permanently available to me although seldom in the forefront of my mind.

Secondly, why should stability be seen as a source of intrinsic value anyway? If it means durability, as we have been supposing, it could be a nuisance. I wanted to know what time the film I was going to see was on; but I certainly don't want to retain that knowledge indefinitely; when it has served its purpose, let it go! In fact, I must have acquired thousands of items of temporarily useful knowledge at various times, all of which, happily, have run away "like Daedalus' statues"; and a good thing too. The inability to forget things can be a serious *disability*. Perhaps the truth is that the lofty conception of knowledge which we discussed in Chapter 1 underlies Plato's notion of tethering here, so that trivial although occasionally useful items, like the route to Larissa or the time of the film, don't count as bits of knowledge. Or perhaps we need another interpretation of the metaphor of tethering.

The *Theaetetus* account

Plato's most mature thoughts about knowledge are contained in his *Theaetetus*, in form a classic Socratic enquiry of the kind whose rationale is supposedly provided by the theory of recollection in the *Meno*. Theaetetus, described as a gifted young man, is challenged to say what knowledge is. He makes a number of proposals, each of which is tested by means of a Socratic interrogation; none of them stands up to scrutiny and at the end of the day we are left to console ourselves with the thought that at least we have learnt something: that we don't (yet) know what knowledge is. This, it will be remembered from the episode with the slave, is a better state to be in than wrongly thinking that you do know what it is. So some progress has been made: an error has been removed and you have been made aware of the need for further enquiry.

Theaetetus' first suggestion is that knowledge may be equated with perception (*Theaetetus* 151e). The investigation to which this proposal gives rise is by far the longest and the most elaborate in the dialogue. Socrates' task is to work with Theaetetus in developing this simple-seeming suggestion into something like a proper philosophical theory, and then to examine its credentials. Socrates is the midwife who must help bring Theaetetus' philosophical infant to birth and then help to decide whether it is a truly viable infant or "a wind-egg" (*Theaetetus* 148e–151e).

There is at least a superficial plausibility in Theaetetus' first suggestion. Perception is very important to us and we obviously rely on it for much of our information about the world. I step into the garden and feel a chill wind blowing about my ears. In doing so I become apprised of a fact – I get to know that there's a cold wind blowing – and perhaps, before I set off for town, I put on a hat and coat. This seems to be a perfectly clear case of a very common type of knowledge.

But things are not quite so simple. Plato's discussion leads us on a winding route through the philosophical theories of his most eminent predecessors and we shall not follow his course in detail. But there are some salient points we need to note. First, he puts a typically ironic spin on the suggestion that knowledge is perception. The most obvious point about knowledge is contained in the truism which we highlighted in Chapter 1: if you know, you can't be wrong; knowing that P requires that P be true. If we bear this in mind, Plato suggests, we can see how amazingly apt is the idea that knowledge is perception. Take the case of the breeze (Plato's own example). I feel it is cold, and so I say that it is cold. You, on the other hand, feel it is warm, and that is what you say. So we apparently disagree. Disagreements of this sort are notoriously hard to resolve. But perhaps the truth is that we are *both* right. The breeze *is* cold (for me) and it *is* warm (for you) and there is no more to be said. So, in perceptual matters like this, we both satisfy the prime condition for knowing: if you know, you can't be wrong. But if this is what the identification of knowledge with perception involves, there is a heavy price to pay. If neither of us is wrong about how the wind is, and we apply apparently contrary epithets to it, it follows that there is no *objective* truth of the matter (the epithets are not really contrary). Plato's thought is that Theaetetus' proposed identification of knowledge in general with perception leads directly into the relativism taught by Protagoras and popularly sloganized as saying "Man [or, perhaps it would be better to translate, '*a* man'] is the measure of all things"; Plato represents Protagoras as saying, more formally, "as each thing appears to me, so it is for me, and as it appears to you, so it is for you – you and I each being a man" (*Theaetetus* 152a).

Protagorean doctrines have always had advocates, not least at the dawn of the twenty-first century. They are especially appealing in the domain of values, where disagreements are particularly hard to resolve and there can be no appeal to scientifically attested fact. It may well seem that on some questions we can only agree to differ. One of us admires 12-tone music and another regards it as a terrible cultural aberration. One of us feels that suicide may sometimes be a sensible and morally acceptable course of action, while another holds it in abhorrence. What are we to say? At the end of the day, perhaps all we can do is agree to differ. But what lies behind this agreement to differ? Is it that there is *in principle* nothing else to do because there is no objective truth in the matter? What seems right or good to me (after careful reflection, perhaps) *is* right or good (for me). And if it seems bad to you, then it *is* bad (for you). Or is it that it is more socially acceptable, more comfortable, to agree to differ and get on with other things because the truth is very hard to find?

For Plato, at least, the defence of objectivity is the overriding priority, even though the truth may be very hard to find. Any form of relativism or subjectivism is utter anathema to him. Three strands of thought become salient in the subsequent discussion.

To begin with, the Protagorean theory is at odds with deeply engrained and pervasive aspects of everyday thinking which we noted earlier. If no sincerely held opinion is ever wrong, then no one is more knowledgeable, more expert, than anyone else. So why should you go to the *doctor* when you are ill? On this view of things, there is no sense in which a doctor's opinion is to be preferred to any old charlatan's, or to your own, if you have one. In fact, of course, rightly or wrongly, we do expect doctors to know better than others how our illnesses will develop and may perhaps be cured or our symptoms alleviated; we do think some people are quacks, and most of us are pretty modest about our own diagnostic powers. The idea of available expertise is deeply engrained in us. We expect the chef to know how the dish will turn out, the mechanic to understand why the car doesn't start, the horticulturist to be able to advise us about what plants will thrive in our soil, and so on. In general, we think that some people's opinions on some matters are more deserving of attention and respect than others'. Indeed, this is one of the ways in which the preference for knowledge over mere opinion, which Meno challenged us to explain, is expressed. The idea that truth is independent of individual points of view, that some people know better than others about particular matters and that some people may be plain wrong, is all but impossible for us to give up. The Protagorean theory would undermine it, but in fact it fails to dislodge us from these ordinary ways of thinking. Moreover, and this is Plato's second point against Protagoras, the theory seems to defeat itself. I am not convinced by Protagoras' teaching; I think it is wrong. But this means that its advocates must accept that it *is* wrong: wrong for me, that is, although not wrong for them.

The crucial point, however, on which, as Plato thinks, Theaetetus' Protagorean equation of knowledge with perception finally founders, is deeper and more subtle. He puts it in the following way:

> SOCRATES   Take a sound and a colour. First of all don't you think this same thing about both of them, namely that they both are?
>
> THEAETETUS   I do.
>
> SOCRATES   Also that each of them is different from the other and the same as itself? . . . And that both together are two, and each of them is one?
>
> THEAETETUS   Yes I think that too.
>
> . . .
>
> SOCRATES   Now what is it through which you think all these things about them? It is not possible, you see, to grasp what is common to both either through sight or through hearing. . . .
>
> THEAETETUS   I couldn't possibly say. All I can tell you is that it doesn't seem to me that for these things there is any special instrument at all, as there is for the others. It seems to me that in investigating the common features of everything the soul functions through itself.   (*Theaetetus* 185a–e)

Plato's point is put in a manner that sounds strangely in our ears. The idea is that many of our judgements, including those about perceptual properties, transcend what is actually given in perception; there are elements in what we say when we express these judgements that cannot be accounted for by referring to the sensory input we have received. Appreciations of samenesses and differences, of existence and non-existence, or of numerosity, are not attributable to any *particular* sense-modality, since they occur with reference to *all* sense-modalities and across different sense-modalities. Even a blind/deaf person who has no idea how red things look or how middle C sounds is not precluded from knowing that red is *one* property and sounding middle C when struck a *different* property. The thesis that knowledge *is* perception cannot account for such knowledge. (In his time, Kant (1724–1804) was to argue that knowledge requires the application of very general category-concepts, which are part of the innate structure of minds, to the jumble of sense-perceptions.)

This idea, that knowledge transcends sensory perception, is a recurrent theme in philosophy. In recent times it has been explored in a new way. Suppose that my cat is gazing intently at a small bird in the garden. There is no reason to doubt that it *sees* the bird – after all, it is preparing to pounce on it. But shall we say that in seeing the bird in the garden it sees *that* the bird *is* in the garden or *that there is* a bird in the garden? These latter formulae, which are of a very common type, are used to ascribe what has been called "epistemic seeing" (Dretske 1969: passim). What they ascribe is knowledge, or at least beliefs, fed by, but not the same as, episodes of "non-epistemic" seeing. My cat certainly sees (non-epistemically) a bird in the garden. It is not blind; the bird is within its field of vision and there is reason to think that the cat's attention is focused on it. This is, so to speak, raw perception. Perhaps it also has some beliefs; some philosophers will not scruple to say so although others may deny it. If it is claimed that it has some belief, it may be convenient to describe this as the belief that there is a bird in front of it, even perhaps a bird in the garden. But that description derives from our need to find a way of identifying the belief we want to ascribe. We might just as well identify it as the belief that there is food (or fun, or prey) to be had. My cat lacks the conceptual resources to frame such thoughts for itself. So if we were to say that it can *see that* there is a bird in the garden we should need to be clear that we are using our conceptual resources to identify the belief we are crediting it with rather than claiming it is entertaining a belief under that very description. All we can really be sure of is that it is visually aware of what *we* would describe as a bird in the garden. To say, without qualification, that it *sees that* there is a bird in the garden is to credit it with more than we can sensibly attribute to our pets: articulate judgement that involves applying concepts which are not given in the perception. It is to enter the world of Peter Rabbit and Mrs Tiggy-Winkle.

Another example. Under certain circumstances, a baby (or a cat) may correctly be said to smell escaping gas; it wrinkles its nose, perhaps, or displays some other sign of olfactory distress. But it cannot be correct to say flatly that it smells *that there is* an escape of gas, since it is entirely ignorant about gas and the possibility of gas leaks. The baby does not judge on the basis of its olfactory experience that there is a gas leak. There is no reason to think it judges at all. But, of course, it smells something.

Let us now return to the breeze, where Plato's discussion of knowledge and perception begins. Disputes about how cold or warm the weather is are notoriously fruitless. If I were to insist, contrary to what you say, that the wind *is* cold, and not just cold *for me* (whatever that is supposed to mean), I should be claiming it as an objective fact that it is cold; by implication I should be claiming that you were wrong about the fact. Assuming that you are not mistaken about how the wind feels to you (how could you be?), it follows that your error lies elsewhere. You are mistaken in claiming to know the temperature of the wind. So a wedge is driven between perception and judgement. But the breeze provides a good case for Theaetetus' equation of knowledge with perception just because here it is fruitless to get into these disputes. For Greeks who (I surmise) had no independent means of measuring temperature, wind-chill factors and so on, it seems likely there was no way of resolving them.

Knowledge and the judgements in which it is expressed always transcend what is actually given through the senses, and Theaetetus' equation cannot stand. Plato, perhaps, would go further than this; he certainly did in the *Republic*. In *Republican* mood, he would deny even the possibility of objective judgements based on or about what is perceived; to put it another way, he would deny the very possibility of so-called epistemic *seeing* (or epistemic any of the other sense-modalities). And, in the *Theaetetus*, he finds it helpful, while developing the Protagorean view he credits Theaetetus with, to sketch a theory about the nature of perception that makes the terms we use to express definite judgements completely inapplicable in the domain of the senses. This is the theory of Heraclitus, sloganized by saying that everything is in a state of flux, or all things are flowing. Heraclitus pictures the world as a swirl of movement; nothing is fixed or still. "I" have no fixed identity, despite what this use of the pronoun suggests. And the "things" that "I" perceive have no fixed identity either. "My" perceptions are generated from the interactions of the ever-changing swirl that "I" refer to as "me" and the ever-changing swirl out there. On this view, it is never possible to say with truth that something in the material world *is* the case. Any ascription of a stable property or state freezes what is essentially fluid.

So much for Theaetetus' proposed equation of knowledge with perception. We are now firmly embarked on a typical Socratic enquiry. One initially quite attractive-seeming suggestion as to what knowledge might be has been discredited. In the terms suggested by the *Meno*, after some argument and reflection our faded recollection of what knowledge is has been sharpened sufficiently to allow us to see that the definition of knowledge as perception cannot be right. This definition cannot accommodate our intuitions about objectivity.

Perhaps, so Theaetetus now suggests, knowledge just *is* true judgement or true belief; that's how it transcends the contingencies of the particular sense-modalities. Plato immediately finds a profound difficulty connected with this suggestion, which I shall now outline, but which I shall not investigate in detail; disentangling Plato's highly sophisticated muddles, if that is what they are, would take us too far off course. The difficulty is this. We have discovered that we operate with a notion of objectivity, entrenched in our very idea of knowledge, such that what seems to me to be the case may not actually be the case. I can be wrong. My beliefs can be false. I am not the ultimate authority. And our theory of knowledge needs to allow for this possibility. But Plato finds it hard to understand how it is possible to have a false belief. If I believe falsely that P, then I have something that is not the case in mind, or, in Plato's own terminology, I have *what is not* in mind. But how can this be? What is not, is not: it seems there is nothing to *be* in my mind, nothing to *be* an object of my belief. Clearly, we need to work out a theory of belief, an account of how it is structured, that will leave space for the possibility of believing what is not. Plato tries out several different models but they all fail and, in the end, this particular, technical problem is set aside. We shall also set it aside.

So we are left with the suggestion that knowledge is true belief or true judgement. But this idea is rather easily discredited by means of a single counter-example (*Theaetetus* 201a–c). We can imagine how a lawyer might, by eloquence and clever advocacy, persuade a jury of something that just happens to be true. He cannot *teach* what happened in a case of mugging, because there are no eyewitnesses he can call on, but he is eloquent enough to *persuade* the audience of what happened. The audience will not end up with knowledge in this instance but they will end up believing what is true. There is some controversy over just how Plato's thought runs here; the main lines, however, are clear. The advocate is in no position to teach, but he is a skilled persuader. Rhetorical persuasion generates beliefs, but does not, as teaching can, impart knowledge. In the case in question, the belief happens to be true, but being only the product of persuasion cannot amount to knowledge. Knowledge of matters like this, so Plato says, requires the evidence of the senses; an eyewitness, and only an eyewitness, could tell us what happened.

There are two ideas running here. One is that rhetorical persuasion cannot impart knowledge. It goes with belief, opinion; knowledge can only be imparted by teaching. The other is the idea which, as we noted earlier, goes clean against Plato's teaching in the *Republic*, and even the theory of perception developed earlier in the *Theaetetus* – that some kinds of knowledge require sensory evidence. It is the first point that carries the burden of argument here; it is a recurrent theme in Plato that clever persuasion, whether practised in the law courts or by johnny-come-lately sophists with facile recipes for living successful lives, can *never* instil knowledge.

Assuming that the counter-example is cogent, we must now look for another definition of knowledge. And here we come at last to the first properly developed proposal for a tripartite analysis of knowledge. Theaetetus introduces the idea that knowledge is true judgement with *logos*, while true judgement which is *logos*-less is outside the domain of knowledge. Possession of a *logos* is what makes the difference between someone who has only been persuaded that P by a clever talker and someone who has been properly taught that P and learnt their lesson. The remainder of the dialogue tests three interpretations of this idea, none of which is found to be satisfactory. *Logos* is a difficult, extremely common and very versatile word. It is hard to translate univocally. Sometimes it means simply *word*; that is how it is usually translated at the beginning of John's Gospel in the New Testament: "In the beginning was the Word". More often it means things like reason, account, explanation or calculation. It is, of course, related to the word *logismos*, in the phrase *aitias logismos* in the *Meno*: whatever it is that, according to that account, tethers beliefs so as to make them knowledge.

In the *Theaetetus*, Plato ask whether the thought is, first, that a person with a true belief has knowledge if she can spell out her belief in words. No, that would be far too generous, including practically everyone who has a true belief (*Theaetetus* 206d1–e4). Secondly, could the difference be that, unlike the person who only has a true belief, the person with knowledge can specify all the elements in what she knows? No; if you just happen to hunch that Theaetetus' name is spelt T-H-E-A-E-T-E-T-U-S, you won't *know* how to spell it even though you will have specified all the right elements in the right order (*Theaetetus* 207a1–208b12). Thirdly and lastly, might the idea be that the knower, unlike the mere true believer, is able to specify some distinctive mark of the thing she knows? No; if I have no idea at all how Theaetetus differs from other individuals, how could I even have a (true) belief about *him*, as distinct from anyone else (*Theaetetus* 208c–210a10)?

On this inconclusive note the dialogue ends. We are left at least with a clear appreciation that we don't yet know clearly what knowledge is. In particular we don't know whether some other tripartite analysis might not be correct: perhaps one with a different interpretation of *logos*. Alternatively, perhaps we should abandon the thought that knowledge is necessarily a matter of true *belief* (opinion or judgement). What seems inconceivable is that Plato ever gave up on the thought that there is an essence of knowledge, an essence which could, at least in principle, be captured in some formula (*logos*). The whole of his philosophy is driven by the thought that there are such essences and the task of philosophy is to bring them to light. The theory of Forms is a theorization of this conviction. The same thought (although differently rationalized) has animated more recent attempts to find an account of what knowledge is and superficially they have often followed the same pattern of Plato's failed shot in the *Theaetetus*. The motivation, however, has generally been very different from Plato's, as we shall see.

Analysing knowledge
3 the modern way

Preamble

Plato was an optimist about knowledge: he believed it could be attained and could be taught to other people. To be sure, in the *Republic* at any rate, he believed it was beyond the capacities of most of us; but the élite in his republic, the so-called philosophers or philosopher cadets, have both the intellectual power and the right disposition to acquire it. What they need is the right schooling. In the end, in his valedictory work on the topic, he is unable to find a satisfactory account of what exactly knowledge is, and he never adequately works out how essentially subjective states of belief relate to, or perhaps transmute into, knowledge of objective realities. But this does not undermine his faith in the possibility of knowledge; it is the proper and achievable goal of all philosophical enquiry. The Academy that he founded was the practical expression of this vision: an institution where knowledge could be pursued cooperatively and cultivated in others.

Descartes, too, believed that, under God, the rational intellect could gain an infallible insight into truth. But he reached this position by a very different route from Plato's. As mentioned in the Introduction, he was greatly influenced by the recently rediscovered writings of the ancient sceptics. These philosophers had specialized in the development of arguments that were designed to subvert all beliefs. Their overall purpose, however, was not nihilistic but therapeutic. Reflection on sceptical arguments was thought to provide a kind of meditative technique for dealing with negative feelings. The technique was supposed to work by systematically undermining beliefs. The idea was that a life lived without beliefs would be a contented one. If you have no beliefs, you will not risk disappointments, and you will have no cause for fear or anxiety. It is extremely hard for us to think ourselves into the mind-set of these sceptics, but there is no doubt that they were in earnest. Hume, a century after Descartes, was fascinated by their ideas, and perfectly sums up our common-sense reaction: if scepticism, of the ancient sort, really took off, he tells us, "All discourse, all action would immediately cease; and men remain in a total lethargy, till the necessities of nature, unsatisfied, put an end to their miserable existence" (1975: XII.ii, 159).

Happily, so Hume thought, we *cannot* adhere to a sceptical position. However good sceptical arguments may be, it is contrary to our nature as human beings that we should believe their conclusions. Perhaps the arguments, considered *as* arguments, are rationally cogent. Hume certainly thought they were. But they fail to carry conviction, and the fact that they fail in this regard shows conclusively that the controls on our beliefs are not rational; according to Hume they are "natural". This is the moral he wants us to draw. As he puts it in his *Treatise*, "Nature, by an absolute and uncontrollable necessity has determined us to judge as well as to breathe and feel" (1978: I, iv, i, 183).

Descartes, a century earlier, had also thought the arguments for scepticism were very powerful and he develops a representative selection of some of the most telling ones in his *Meditations* and elsewhere. But Descartes is not a sceptic either. His driving thought is that each of us can use sceptical argument to excise from the body of her beliefs any which are vulnerable to even the faintest shadow of theoretical doubt. From here on, well-founded certainty that one is not wrong is apt to be seen as a condition for *knowing* something. Famously, Descartes recommends to his readers the following overriding argument (which, in various hyped-up forms, can be found in many, more recent books): for all I can know to the contrary, there is a powerful and supernatural being bent on making me go unwittingly wrong in all the ways it can, so perhaps any of my beliefs may be in error and there is nothing I can confidently believe. (Or, in modern versions, perhaps I am a brain kept in a vat of nutrient fluid, stimulated to have the experiences, the feelings, emotions and beliefs that I do at the whim of a mad scientist.) Descartes thinks a good philosophical strategy for me (and for anyone) will be to work on the assumption that there is such a malign demon out to deceive me. The idea is that if any of my beliefs turn out to be immune to this hypothetical demon's most determined machinations, then these beliefs may provide the secure foundation of a body of future knowledge; and, of course, he thought there was one such belief. Hence the celebrated observation, "*I am, I exist*, is necessarily true whenever it is put forward by me or conceived in my mind" (*2nd Meditation*).

Descartes thought that once I appreciate *how* I am certain of this incontrovertible truth, I will see that I can, with the aid of a bit of argument, be certain in just the same way and to the same degree that God also exists – God who, by his very nature, *will not* deceive me. Secure in this knowledge, I can then seek further truths, equally clear and certain, and thus establish a body of knowledge that is safe from the sceptic. If I fall into error, that will be on account of my own carelessness. I can be sure that there is no demon, but a benevolent and all-powerful God who has made it possible for me to achieve truth with certainty. I must be quite ruthless, however, in withholding assent from anything that I do not perceive to be true *very clearly and distinctly*, for that is how God marks out the truth for me.

The power of an argument with this structure has been questioned from the time it was first conceived. I cannot doubt that I exist. Reflection reveals that I cannot doubt it in virtue of the clarity and distinctness with which I apprehend this fact whenever I turn my mind to the question of my existence; this gives me my paradigm of certain, indubitable apprehension. In the same clear and distinct way, after a bit of argument, I apprehend the existence of a God who will not cause me to fall into error: in other words, the very God who *guarantees* that what I apprehend clearly and distinctly is true. Here Descartes seems to be arguing in a circle, using an argument to establish the existence of the God who guarantees the soundness of the argument that is used to establish God's existence. Descartes denied that he was embroiled in a *vicious* circle, but the status of his reasoning has remained a matter of controversy ever since it was first propounded, and, I suppose, the very existence of controversy means that the Cartesian system, in which this is an essential element, lacks the absolutely compelling rational force that Descartes aspired to.

Nonetheless, his adoption of sceptical argument as a way of filtering out uncertainty from the body of our beliefs has cast a very long shadow over the subsequent history of philosophy. If Plato was primarily moved by the desire for understanding and a concern with securing a notion of objectivity, Descartes and his successors up to our own time are as much moved by the desire to establish certainty. Justified certainty, along with truth, has, it seems, become the touchstone of knowledge. An important aspect of this approach is that epistemology has acquired a strongly individualistic slant. In the post-Cartesian world, each of us must strive to maximize certainty for herself; anything we get from books and the testimony of other people is suspect. We should never resign our judgement to others. It is, of course, no accident that Descartes developed his ideas at a time when the medieval world-view, heavily dependent on the supposedly authoritative teachings of Aristotle and Ptolemy, was beginning to disintegrate. That medieval view Berkeley (1685–1753) famously mocked, some years later than Descartes, when he wrote of the close and immediate connection that "custom may establish betwixt the very word *Aristotle* and the motions of assent and reverence in the minds of men" (Berkeley 1710: Introduction xx). Descartes, for his part, despised all book learning. Thus he remarks in his *Discourse on the Method (Part 1)*,

> as soon as I was old enough to emerge from the control of my teachers, I entirely abandoned the study of letters. Resolving to seek no knowledge other than that which could be found in myself or else in the great book of the world I spent the rest of my youth travelling . . . (1985: 115)

Descartes made important and lasting contributions to mathematics, but, unfortunately, his ambition to establish a body of certain knowledge about the physical universe, proof against sceptical argument, was not realized. As we have seen, the argument that is meant to underpin the whole system is, at best, controversial. Moreover, his physics was soon supplanted by Newton's very differently conceived science; and, in any case, the idea that physics might be rooted in theology, although no doubt attractive to some people, no longer has the general appeal that perhaps it had in Descartes's time. No one nowadays, I daresay, is a full-blooded

Cartesian. But Descartes's concern with immunizing us against scepticism, with maximizing certainty, continues to be a live concern. It is not much of an exaggeration to say that the pursuit of certainty has largely obscured other ways of addressing problems about the nature of knowledge. It is, for one example, completely explicit in Ayer (1910–89) (Ayer 1956).

Modern philosophers of knowledge, who still mostly work in the shadow of Descartes's demon, are obliged to find new ways of securing certainty. This is the context in which we need to understand modern tripartite analyses of knowledge. The prevailing modern conception of knowledge is that of true beliefs which are somehow maximally secured against doubt; the problem is to find the formula that adequately conveys how the beliefs are to be secured if they are to count as knowledge. An incidental consequence of this stance is that modern discussions of scepticism are not, like the ancient discussions, concerned with believing as such but rather with the possibility of knowing. So far as believing is concerned we are all perhaps Humeans; we can, no doubt, be dislodged from particular beliefs by means of fresh evidence, argument and so on, but the idea that we could be induced to give up believing *in general* strikes us as completely absurd. But, if there are no beliefs that can be adequately secured against doubt, perhaps there is no such thing as knowledge. Hence the intense focus, in epistemology, on the problem of immunizing beliefs against error.

Methodological matters

How, then, is a modern philosopher to set about the task of providing an account of what knowledge is? How are true beliefs to be secured against doubt so as to qualify as knowledge? In practice, it may appear, most philosophers who have addressed this question have actually followed in Plato's footsteps. They have started from the fundamental Platonic assumption that there is a single essence of knowledge which might be captured in a more or less succinct definition, usually expressed as a list of the separately necessary and jointly sufficient conditions for the truth of a proposition of the form "A knows that P". And they have proceeded, in the Socratic style of many of Plato's dialogues, to test out intuitively plausible hypotheses as to what the definition of knowledge might be, successively abandoning or amending their hypotheses in the light of examples that intuition reveals as *counter*-examples until they have satisfied themselves that they have discovered a definition (*the* definition) which is proof against further counter-examples. Plato had a theory which underpins and validates this procedure. As we have seen from his treatment of Meno's Paradox, he conceives of the dialectical process of testing and amending proposed definitions as one in which latent knowledge, gathered in some other mode of existence, is reawakened and brought to light. Modern practitioners of the method, however, do not carry their Platonism into his metaphysical realm. So what sort of theoretical underpinnings do they have in mind for their procedures?

The question is not asked often enough, but, perhaps, the following sketch of an answer would be generally accepted. The enquirer, seeking to give an account of what knowledge is (or what justice is, what virtue is, etc.), does indeed proceed, as Plato suggests, by summoning up intuitions to test hypotheses, and in doing so she is drawing on resources of latent knowledge that she already possesses. But this is not knowledge gained, as Plato thought, in some different mode of existence; it is ordinary linguistic know-how, picked up in the process of acquiring the language we share. We know the truth-conditions for propositions of the form "A knows that P" to just the extent that we have mastered the use of the English word *know* and its cognates. In trying to give a philosophical account of knowledge, we are in effect trying to articulate the rules with which we operate when we use the word. Notoriously, this kind of project is not easy. It is one thing to speak a language and quite another thing to formulate in explicit detail the rules to which one adheres in speaking it. Perhaps this is the truth behind Augustine's (354–430) often quoted remark in the *Confessions*: "What, then, is time? If no one asks me, I know; if I wish to explain it to one that asketh, I know not" (Gale 1968: 40).

This account of philosophical enquiry makes it seem a much more humdrum and less exhilarating project than Plato's: glorified lexicography, in fact. But it is more than just that. For one thing, the motivation is quite different. The philosopher of this stamp, unlike the lexicographer, is not interested in unravelling the rules that govern the use of just any word. She focuses on those words whose uses may be seen as exercises of concepts which are of particular interest and importance to us: knowledge, justice, reason, freedom and so on. Moreover, it isn't really the *words* that interest her, but rather the shared ideas which are represented by the words of our language and, it seems likely, of other languages, too. And her aspiration is to enlarge our self-understanding by means of her analysis, while perhaps also dispelling some of the perplexities about these topics that have always tended to bug reflective people – showing the fly the way out of the fly-bottle, as Wittgenstein (1889–1951) once put it (Wittgenstein 1953: 1, 308).

But how is this philosopher to defend her assumption that there is a single essence of knowledge? Plato's essentialism is underpinned by a metaphysical theory concerning the essences he hoped to uncover. In the absence of a metaphysical theory like his, however, what reason might there be to expect a univocal account of the concept of knowledge? Wittgenstein, for his part, famously viewed the assumption that it will always be possible to find a unitary account of any given word as a philosophical superstition, which he refers to as the "craving for generality":

> We are inclined to think that there must be something in common to all games, say, and that this common property is the justification for applying the general term "game" to the various games; whereas games form a *family* the members of which have family likenesses. Some of them have the same nose, others the same eyebrows and others again the same way of walking; and these likenesses overlap. The idea of a general concept being a common property of its particular instances connects up with other primitive, too simple, ideas of the structure of language. It is comparable to the idea that *properties* are *ingredients* of the things which have the properties; e.g. that beauty is an ingredient of all beautiful things, as alcohol is of beer and wine, and that we therefore could have pure beauty, unadulterated by anything that is beautiful.
>
> (1953: 1, 17)

(The last sentence, of course, refers to Plato.) Now, as it is for the word *game*, according to Wittgenstein, so perhaps it might be for the word *knowledge* and its cognates. At all events the essentialist presumption of much modern work in the philosophy of knowledge should not be allowed to go unquestioned.

Wittgenstein's suggestions about family likenesses in fact impact on the philosophy of knowledge in at least two ways. First, it has become customary to distinguish radically different varieties of knowledge. It is, so we are often told, one kind of thing to know that the queen is in her castle and quite another kind of thing to know the queen. Knowledge of the latter kind cannot be analysed or decomposed into knowledge of the former sort, nor vice versa. It may well be the case that no one could know the queen who did not also know a number of factual propositions about her. But, on the one hand, we cannot specify which factual propositions Jane knows in knowing the queen; the list seems to be quite indeterminate. And, on the other hand, whatever factual propositions about the queen Jane knows, exactly those propositions could also be known by John without its being the case that *he* knows the queen. Here we are contrasting what Bertrand Russell (1872–1970) called knowledge of truths and knowledge of things (including, of course, people) (Russell 1959: 44). Other distinctions have also been urged. Gilbert Ryle (1900–1976), for example, insisted on a difference between *knowing that* (knowledge of truths) and *knowing how* (Ryle 1949: 125–61). Again, it seems unlikely that "Joan knows how to swim" might be analysed out into a (possibly indeterminate) series of "Joan knows that . . ." propositions: unlikely, at least, where "Joan knows how to swim" is more or less equivalent to "Joan can swim". In some contexts, however, perhaps *knowing how* does decompose into *knowing that*. At all events, if someone asserts that they know how an internal combustion engine works, we should expect them to be able to explain their knowledge by giving a description of the mechanical processes involved, aided, perhaps, with diagrams; no doubt, some people will be able to give a more fluent description than others, but then this is a fact about them rather than about the kind of knowledge they possess.

It seems that many modern philosophers of knowledge, faced with these distinctions between apparently different kinds of knowledge, have been happy to abandon the search for an element common to them all. In fact, they have been predominantly interested in factual knowledge and, for the most part, have been content to let the rest go hang, so that the question of how factual knowledge may be related to Russell's knowledge of things, or to Ryle's knowing how, has rarely been considered. But perhaps they have not always taken on board what Wittgenstein's suggestion about family likenesses may be taken to imply. I think it is implausible to suggest that the word *know* is radically equivocal in the way that the word *bank*, for example, is often said to be (bank of a stream vs. institution for the safekeeping of money). Perhaps these different uses of the word *know* really are members of *one* family. If so, then, surely we may ask, what makes this so? To put it another way, what makes these different uses of *know* different applications of a single concept? Perhaps there is no common feature in all the instances, but if they form a family should we not expect there to be some genetic relationships which we can try to plot? This seems to me to be a proper aspiration for a philosopher of knowledge, although I shall not attempt to realize it in this book. It looks like an evasion to say flatly that there are just different senses of the word *know*, and that's that.

In fact, most recent philosophers of knowledge have focused exclusively on knowledge of truths (alternatively called "factual knowledge" or – more contentiously, at least for those influenced by Zeno Vendler (Vendler 1972: Ch. 5) – "propositional knowledge") and I shall, hereafter, follow them in this. This brings us to the second way the notion of family likenesses impacts on the philosophy of knowledge. We should ask whether it is really appropriate to look, as so many do, for a *common* essence in all instances of factual knowledge or in all those uses of *know* and its cognates that refer to factual knowledge. Perhaps *knowing that* is itself a family likeness term. Here, too, it seems to me right that we should seek to explain how the various uses of *know* in the context of factual knowledge can be exercises of a single concept; but we should be cautious about assuming that the explanation is going to consist in the discovery of a single common feature: the essence, supposedly expressible as a list of the necessary and sufficient conditions for ascribing factual knowledge. We should also be wary of assuming that the concept of knowledge is only ever deployed when the word *know* or its cognates are used. I am going to argue that the concept of knowledge is often in the air when the word is absent. And I am (in Chapter 6) going to propose a very different kind of way of seeking to understand what knowledge is.

Now, whatever theoretical assumptions are thought to underlie their practice, modern philosophers, as we have seen, regularly develop their analyses of knowledge by consulting their intuitions about when it would be right or wrong to use the word *know* and its cognates. Unfortunately, their consultations are often at best perfunctory, and sometimes of doubtful relevance. We are going to be concerned, for the most part, with modern variants of the tripartite analysis, which says, it will be remembered, that A knows that P if and only if:

1. A believes that P.
2. P is true.
3. A's belief that P is . . .

The proper completion of the third clause has always been seen as the serious problem, so relatively little attention has been given to the first two clauses. And, perhaps, the second at any rate needs little in the way of justification, although it is important to be aware that factual knowledge can be, and frequently is, ascribed in sentences that do not actually identify the proposition whose truth is required if the ascription of knowledge is to be correct. If it is said, truly, "John knows where the cat is", the hearer is left in the dark as to what the proposition is which, on this analysis, John believes in knowing where the cat is; nevertheless, there will be some definite proposition which, on this analysis, he believes to be true and which, on any analysis, must be true if he knows where the cat is. Even so, it may not be the case that John himself can articulate that proposition; perhaps he's an 18-month-old child who is as yet unable to formulate such a sentence as "The cat is in the laundry basket", but whose behaviour can demonstrate that he is fully aware of the fact which that sentence states.

The first clause of the analysis, however, should be seen as more controversial if only because, historically, since the time of *Republican* Plato, knowledge and belief have often been thought to be categorially different; if that were right it could not be the case that knowledge is some form of (suitably qualified) belief or that knowing entails believing. There can be no recipe for making chalk into cheese. In fact, though, this clause is often defended in a very sketchy way. Here are some examples:

Suppose Sam and Alfred both come to have precisely the same reasons for believing that Smith killed Jones. Moreover, suppose that Smith did kill Jones, and that the reasons for believing this are virtually impeccable (perhaps there are several highly reliable eyewitnesses). Sam comes to believe that Smith killed Jones, whereas Alfred does not come to have this belief. Alfred, let us suppose, is a good friend of Smith's and, despite his good reasons, simply does not believe that Smith did such a thing. Sam knows that Smith killed Jones, but Alfred does not, even though Alfred has all the reasons that Sam has. This points to another requirement for factual knowledge, namely that a person can be said to know that *h* only if the person believes that *h*.   (Swain 1981: 22)

The idea behind this rigmarole is that the only substantive difference between Sam and Alfred is that Sam believes, and Alfred does not believe, that Smith did the deed. Intuition, it seems, is supposed to tell us that, in the circumstances described, Sam knows and Alfred doesn't; so, we may infer, it is the presence or absence of belief that makes the difference between knowing and not knowing. But even allowing that intuition does tell us that the one knows and the other doesn't (an intuition which perhaps not everyone will share), in the case as described it is far from evident that it is the absence of belief that accounts for Alfred's not knowing what Sam knows. It might be that Alfred's friendship with Smith prevents him from taking the reasons fully on board, and that explains our (supposed) reluctance to say that he *knows* that Smith did the deed; coincidentally, perhaps it also helps to explain why he doesn't believe it either. In fact, as it seems to me, this case is not described fully enough to yield any clear and definite intuitions about it. And, given the tale, it is tempting to ask what turns on the decision anyway. It's hard not to think that Swain is already persuaded that the tripartite analysis, in which belief is the core element, is correct in its broad outline: perhaps it is that question-begging conviction which underlies his confidence that in the case described Sam knows and Alfred doesn't.

Here is another, more generalized, intuition, allegedly leading to the same conclusion:

> It would be odd indeed for you to claim to know something but
> deny believing what you allegedly know. Belief seems required
> for propositional knowledge.   (Moser *et al*. 1988: 15)

In this case, the reader is invited to imagine that she is claiming to
know something and to note that in this circumstance she would
also naturally be prepared to affirm that she believes it. We may
grant this. But what follows? It does *not* follow, despite what these
authors say, that believing that P is a condition of *knowing* that P. It
might be. But so far as this argument goes, it might be that believing
that P is only required as a condition of the speaker's *being sincere
in claiming* to know that P.

Furthermore, it is not hard to dream up other cases where our
intuitions may seem to tell *against* the idea that believing that P is a
condition of knowing that P. Take the case of the lazy and diffident
schoolgirl. She has not done her history revision and she is
convinced, after she has done the exam, that she has failed it
dismally. She felt she knew none of the answers. She was faced, let
us suppose, with a series of multiple choice questions, each of
which invited her to select, from a range of five, the correct answer
to a straightforwardly factual question about a historical event; and
she felt sure her choices were mostly ignorant, based entirely on
whim. In the event, however, she scores highly. Her mark makes it
statistically most improbable that her answers really were random.
So what shall we say about her? We may be inclined to say that she
simply didn't realize how much she had learnt and therefore knew.
The best explanation of her success is not chance but that she was
recalling (in the manner described by Plato in the *Meno*) previously
acquired knowledge. If our intuitions take us in this direction, it
may seem that we have a plausible case of knowing without believing. Our schoolgirl did not believe with respect to any of her
chosen answers that they were correct – in fact she felt certain that
mostly they were not – but the plausible explanation of her success
is that she had picked up and retained the knowledge required for
the exam. At least a defender of the first clause of the analysis will
have to defend the possibility that our schoolgirl, asked for the date
of the Battle of Agincourt, might know and thus (according to the
analysis) believe that the Battle was fought in 1415, while not
believing that "1415" is the correct answer to the question she was

posed in the exam. Formally, perhaps such a defence is possible; the proposition she does not believe ("the correct answer is '1415'") is, after all, different from the proposition she supposedly does believe. But it strains intuition to accept this defence, and strained intuitions are not what the analytic methodology requires.

There is a point to be noted about the opposed "intuitions" just mentioned. The intuitions about the schoolgirl are, so to speak, spectator intuitions. We are external commentators on the scene, considering what we should say about her, how we should account for her successful performance. But Moser and his colleagues cite (what they take to be) the subject's own intuition about what that subject would be willing to say about herself in a certain situation: that is, a *reflexive* intuition.

There is a nest of problems about reflexive intuitions; they need to be handled with great circumspection. First, it is all too easy, as already mentioned, to mistake conditions for *saying* "I know . . ." responsibly and sincerely for truth-conditions of what is said. That one believes that P is certainly a condition for being sincere in asserting that one knows that P; it doesn't follow that it is also a condition for the truth of the proposition asserted. Secondly, examples of this sort require us to reflect upon intuitions about "claiming to know": that is, to look into our own souls and see whether we should or should not be prepared to say, in so many words, "I know . . ." under whatever circumstances may be specified. But such intuitions are a poor guide to understanding the concept of knowledge. There are many contexts in which I might claim to know, or at least I might let it be clearly understood that I know, that the cat is on the mat, for example, simply by saying "It's on the mat". This would be the case if I said it flatly without qualification in response to the question "Where's the cat?" We need to be clearly aware that the concept of knowledge may be in the offing, even though the word *know* and its cognates are entirely absent. This is *typically* the case in the context of questions and answers; but it is true in numerous other contexts, too. The station announcer who says, "The 8.45 for London is running 30 minutes late", is letting you know something. And so, for the most part, in intention at least, are the writers of encyclopaedias, dictionaries, textbooks and so on. In fact, it seems pretty evident to me that the concept of knowledge is in the offing in a non-manifest way far more often than in a manifest way. The compilers of encyclopaedias and dictionaries do not normally intersperse their entries with "I know that . . ." or "We know that . . ." or "It is known that . . .", but the tacit assumption is that they are purveying knowledge. So, too, with news reports on radio and television and in the press; so, too, with textbooks and so forth; so, too, as often as not, with gossip. If this is right, it means that those who think to get an insight into the concept of knowledge from consulting intuitions about uses of the word are focusing on a very narrow range of cases; they might do better to attend to intuitions about the second-order descriptions that we find it appropriate to give of our linguistic behaviour in various contexts rather than intuitions about the first-order speech-acts in which the word is used. That policy will give us a much less restricted view of the business of knowledge. It would, for example, reveal that the concept of knowledge is in the air when I flatly reply "Harold" to the question "Which English king was killed at the Battle of Hastings?"; the point of the reply is to let the questioner know that Harold was killed at Hastings or perhaps to satisfy her that I know it was Harold.

Finally, when the word *know* actually is used in a first-order speech-act, there is often a quite special reason for it, and this is especially true when it is used in the first person; reflexive intuitions are particularly liable to mislead. In the first person, for example, it is often used to concede a point – "I *know* that it is raining, but I want to go out all the same" – or, again, it may be used to emphasize that this is the truth of the matter – "I *know* that it's raining, of course I do. I've only just this second come in". Here we need to be careful not to confuse the considerations that may be relevant to using the phrase "I know . . ." with this or that special force, for conditions on knowledge itself. One might think it out of order to use it for emphasis, as in the second of these examples, if one is not 100 per cent certain; it doesn't *follow* (although it might nonetheless be true) that in order to know that P one has to be 100 per cent certain that P.

Now, to return to the tripartite analysis. Once the belief-condition has been granted, one may wonder whether it (along with truth) is sufficient for knowledge. We saw how Plato was persuaded it was not, by citing our intuition that rhetorical persuasion alone, while capable of inducing belief, cannot impart knowledge about the circumstances of a particular crime. Here is a more modern (and more perfunctory) example:

> If one has knowledge, then one also has right or true opinion. But the converse is not true: one may have right or true opinion without having knowledge. Thus we may guess correctly today, and therefore, have true opinion, but not know until tomorrow. (Chisholm 1966: 5)

But who on earth supposes that guessing generates *beliefs* (and lucky-guessing true beliefs)? If that were so, aficionados of the lottery would be cruelly disappointed, week after week, when the outcome turns out to be contrary to their beliefs. In general, of course, what they have is hopes about the outcome, not beliefs.

I have laboured these points not in order to discredit the time-honoured use of intuitions to test the merit of hypotheses about the nature of knowledge, but rather to bring home, with a few examples from quite distinguished philosophers, how important it is to use this method with care. It seems to me that all too often philosophers have used their intuitions not in a genuinely heuristic way, like Plato, but in a kind of pseudo-heuristic fashion, pretending to confirm hypotheses about the nature of knowledge when it is evident that they are already and independently convinced of their truth. There is, perhaps, a lack of symmetry here between the intuitions that are appealed to in order to confirm hypotheses about knowledge and those used to discredit hypotheses. Intuitions that are, like most of Plato's, disconfirmatory often seem to be quite decisive; confirmatory ones, however, on the evidence of the examples given above, are often suspect.

The Gettier problem

In 1963, Edmund Gettier published a brief note in *Analysis* (Gettier 1963). He believed that he had found counter-examples that threatened the very idea of analysing knowledge in terms of justified true belief, or any variant of this formula. His counter-examples work, not by attacking this clause or that clause of the analysis, but by showing that the whole ensemble of proposed clauses could be satisfied and a person still not know that P. In other words, he attacks the sufficiency of the analysis rather than the necessity of any of its components. The subsequent history of the philosophy of knowledge has been, with some notable exceptions, the history of philosophers' attempts to deal with this problem, largely keeping to the spirit of the tripartite form of analysis while trying to immunize it against Gettier-type counter-examples. Sometimes an extra clause has been suggested to neutralize the counter-examples; sometimes the justification-clause has been refined or an alternative formula proposed in its place. It would be tedious to retell the whole of this history. Much of the history, although happily not all of it, is itself rather tedious. This bit of philosophy has tended to take on the appearance of a game: a test of philosophical ingenuity in devising counter-examples to particular analyses and then inventing ways of neutering them within the broad framework of the favoured type of analysis. As a number of commentators have pointed out, it is all a bit reminiscent of Ptolemaic astronomy. Ptolemaic astronomers were determined to preserve the central tenet of Ptolemy's theory at all costs: the earth is at the centre of the universe and the planets move around it in a perfectly regular way. Unfortunately, their accounts of the planetary motions were from time to time undermined by new observations. The strategy then was to keep the core theory, but complicate it in order to accommodate the newly observed phenomena. The upshot was a theory of amazing elaboration, happily destined to be replaced in time by an entirely new and essentially simpler kind of (non-geocentric) theory. So too, perhaps, with the recent history of the philosophy of knowledge. Philosophers became mesmerized by a certain pattern of analysis focused exclusively on the cognitive states of individuals, when really perhaps we need to broaden our horizons and look at things in a radically new way. In the remainder of this chapter I aim to highlight some of the principal moments of the recent history of the philosophy of knowledge. In the following chapters I will make some suggestions about how our horizons might be broadened.

Let us begin with Gettier's proposed counter-examples (slightly elaborated in the interests of verisimilitude):

1. Imagine, then, two people, Smith and Jones, competing for the same job. They have both come for the interview and as part of

the preliminaries they are asked to complete an expenses form. Smith, unfortunately, cannot find his pen and has to borrow Jones's, which he notices to his surprise is a Parker like his own. For Smith, the whole exercise is a bit of a charade, since he has already been told by the Head of the Department that they intend to appoint Jones, who exactly fits the desired profile and has far the stronger curriculum vitae. Nevertheless, at the Head's suggestion, Smith has continued with his application, in order to gain experience of the process. Hence Smith believes, for the best possible reasons, that the person who is going to get the job has a Parker pen with him. And he is right. He is right because he, Smith, is going to get the job. As it turns out he completely outclasses Jones at the interview; and Smith, too, has his Parker pen with him, which, in the stress of the situation, he was unable to find earlier.

Gettier, rightly, thinks it would be counter-intuitive to say that Smith's belief here amounts to knowledge. But the conditions of the tripartite analysis are satisfied. Smith believes that the person who is going to get the job has a Parker pen with him. His belief is true. And he is justified in holding it.

It will be objected perhaps that what Smith really believes is that *Jones* is going to get the job, and this is false. But that proposition together with the proposition that Jones has a Parker pen with him entails, as Smith appreciates, that the person who is going to get the job has a Parker pen with him. And surely, to put it generally, one who is justified in believing that P and appreciates that P entails Q will also be justified in believing that Q. Here is Gettier's second example:

2. We are to imagine that Smith believes, on very good evidence, that Jones owns a Ford. Jones is notorious for never buying any other kind of car – indeed, people are constantly remarking on his dogged faithfulness to the brand – and what is more, Jones has just picked Smith up in a Ford. Smith, reflecting on Jones's addiction to Fords as they drive along, and intermittently brooding about philosophical problems of certainty, recalls an old saying from his childhood and thinks to himself, "Either Jones owns a Ford or I'm a Dutchman". (This curious formula,

it may be recalled, was sometimes used to express a very high degree of certainty in the first of the disjuncts.) Smith then starts idly inventing other similar formulae that one might use for expressing certainty: "Either Jones owns a Ford or pigs can fly", "Either Jones owns a Ford or Jane is in Timbuktu", and so on. Each of these sentences expresses something that Smith firmly believes because he firmly believes that Jones owns a Ford; and if it is true that Jones owns a Ford, then, for any Q, true or false, "Jones owns a Ford or Q" is true. That's the logic exploited by "P or I'm a Dutchman".

The fact of the matter is, however, that Jones does *not* own a Ford. He is driving a hire car. His last car was recently written off in an accident and he hasn't yet replaced it. By a remarkable chance, however, Smith's daughter, Jane, *is* in Timbuktu, her plane having just made an emergency landing, *en route* for South Africa. It follows that in spite of his being wrong about Jones owning a Ford, one of Smith's randomly fabricated disjunctive beliefs is true: "Either Jones owns a Ford or Jane is in Timbuktu". Moreover, he is justified in believing this. Again, surely, our intuition will tell us he does not *know* it.

Now the great game begins: how can we preserve the spirit of the tripartite analysis in the teeth of counter-examples like these? Let us first spell out the principles on which they rely.

First, someone who justifiably believes that P and also correctly notices that P entails Q will also be justified in believing Q; the justification is, so to speak, transmitted through a recognized entailment. This principle seems unexceptionable, and in fact *entailment*, although a feature of Gettier's examples, is perhaps needlessly strong. A subject who justifiably believes that P, and also realizes that P provides good grounds for believing that Q without actually entailing Q, has good grounds for believing that Q. This is a very common structure of reasons. Consider this example from Hume:

A man, who should find in a desert country the remains of pompous buildings, would conclude, that the country had, in ancient times, been cultivated by civilized inhabitants.

(Hume 1975: 45)

This traveller is justified in believing that the stones he confronts are the remains of pompous buildings (P), and from this he infers with good reason that the region was once inhabited by civilized people (Q).

Secondly, it is required that one can be justified in believing something even though it is false. Two points about this. First, and rather trivially, if this were not so, the so-called tripartite analysis would not, strictly speaking, *be* a tripartite analysis since the second clause ("P is true") would not be independent of the third clause, which requires that the subject's belief that P be justified. Secondly, and not so trivially, to suppose that one could only be justified in believing true propositions would be to place an intolerable restriction on the notion of justification. It would mean, for example, that no matter how strong the evidence with which it was presented, a jury could never be justified in delivering a verdict of guilty in the event that the accused was really innocent (or vice versa). But where justice miscarries it is not always thought to be the jury that is at fault; surely they may be justified in delivering the verdict they do, on the evidence they are given, even if the verdict is wrong? Again, Hume's traveller may have drawn a false conclusion. Perhaps the region was always a desert; to be sure, he is right to conclude that there were once some pompous buildings here (P), but these were slave-built follies ordained by the tyrant of a distant city as grandly isolated mausoleums for him and his concubines. But if we were to rule that the traveller's belief lacks justification in the case where it happens to be false, we should also say it lacks justification in the case where it happens to be true; for it is contrary to our intuitions about justification to suppose that chance alone might make the difference between reasons that justify and reasons that don't. If we went down this road, the upshot would be the complete subversion of all inductive argument, since the falsity of any inductive conclusion will always be consistent with the evidence cited in the argument, however strong it may be, and it will always be possible for us, as Hume famously insisted, to imagine a scenario where it *is* false (Hume 1978: 79–80). In fact, Descartes's demon gives us an all-purpose scenario to this end.

One reaction might be to concede that a person may be justified in holding a false belief, but to stipulate that the justifying grounds for a belief must all be true if that belief is to amount to *knowledge*.

In the Gettier examples, a false belief features prominently in Smith's reasoning: in the first case that Jones will get the job and, in the second case, that Jones owns a Ford. Perhaps this is why the beliefs that Smith ends up with, although justified as beliefs, fail to be knowledge; he has justifiably reasoned his way to a correct conclusion, but his reasoning has involved false beliefs along the way. This proposed requirement on knowledge, that the justifying grounds be true, looks plausible but, at least, it needs careful spelling out. We can, for example, imagine a case where Smith has, as it seems to him, a superfluity of evidence for the truth of a proposition (P) that he believes. Much of this evidence is true but some of it is false. There are several subsets of this evidence which contain only true propositions, each of which subsets would be sufficient to justify him in believing P, but there are also a few apparently justifying subsets that contain false propositions. Cases like this may be rather common. Who can say for sure that these conditions are not realized with respect to some of their own beliefs? But it would surely be unduly severe to interpret the principle that knowledge-making justifications have to be error-free in such a way as to disqualify Smith's belief that P merely because he has some false beliefs which, if true, he might properly cite in a knowledge-making justification of his belief.

One response now might be to insist that if his belief that P is to amount to knowledge, none of the false beliefs in his stock of beliefs should actually be *necessary* for him to justify his belief that P; his true beliefs provide him with sufficient justification. But perhaps this is too weak. This condition would be satisfied, after all, even if the justification he actually offers appeals to one of his false beliefs. What matters, it may be said, is not what premises Smith might have available for use, but what premises he actually relies on for his justification. So perhaps the stipulation should be that he doesn't actually use any of his false beliefs in his justification. Unfortunately, in the sort of case described, where Smith has a superfluity of evidence at his command, it is sometimes no easy thing (for him or for us) to determine which premises he actually does use. Should we require that he reason his way explicitly to his conclusion if he is to be justified in holding it? That seems unrealistic; our command of justifications quite often only emerges retrospectively when we are challenged to justify our assertions. Now imagine that Smith, on being retrospectively challenged to justify a belief for which he has a plethora of evidence, produces a false premise. Is this sufficient to warrant our denying that he has knowledge of the fact? That seems hard; after all, when he has the false evidence pointed out to him, he might want to stick with his belief and revise his justification. *Ex hypothesi*, he has plenty of (true) evidence he could draw on. So perhaps we should phrase the requirement in some such way as this: Smith's true belief that P is justified in a manner appropriate to make it knowledge if and only if he has true justificatory evidence at his command which he would rely on under reiterated challenge. This is meant to cover the case just described where he persists in his belief when his initial justification is shown to include some falsity and thereupon offers a new justification.

With some such stipulation as this, can we reinstate the tripartite analysis? Perhaps we can, although anyone who engages with these issues will have pretty good inductive grounds for thinking that sooner or later a counter-example will emerge. And it is, in any event, quite difficult, as the conditions on knowledge are made more elaborate and rarefied, to be sure what one's intuitions are, if indeed one has any that are perfectly unequivocal.

Causal theory

Other approaches to the analysis of knowledge have been tried. The aim, let us remember, has been to find a plausible formula that will ensure that the antecedents of Smith's belief, in the case where it amounts to knowledge, are not contaminated by falsehood. The antecedents we have been considering so far have been any of the sorts of reasons that might ground the belief *for Smith*, any of the reasons that might weigh with him, when he adopts the belief, or when he retrospectively tries to justify it. These are sometimes called "internal reasons": reasons that are contemplated by Smith within the boundaries of his own mind. But there is another class of reasons that may be invoked to explain why people believe what they do. Suppose I believe there is a gecko on the wall of my bedroom. I might believe this for no other reason than that I have been hypnotized into doing so. Hypnotic suggestion would be an *external reason* that explains how it comes about that I believe what

I do: a reason that in itself has nothing to do with how *I* weigh evidence or reach conclusions. It is a wholly external event that impacts on me and my thinking; it causes me to form the belief I do, given a certain triggering event such as my entering my bedroom.

In a case like this there is, surely, no question of my *knowing* that there is a gecko on my wall. More likely than not, there is no gecko there at all; but even if there is, if I believe there is for no other reason than that I have been hypnotized into doing so, I suspect all our intuitions will concur that I do not *know* that there is. (Of course, in this case it might be difficult to sort out whether my having been hypnotized was the only, or the operative, reason why I believed it.) But now consider the case where I believe there is a gecko on the bedroom wall, and the reason is that I can actually see one there. The presence of the gecko on the wall makes me believe that there is a gecko there; my belief is *caused* by its presence. This, too, is an instance where something external to me impacts on me and on my thinking; but in this instance, I suspect that most people, without some philosophical axe to grind, would be happy to say that I *know* there is a gecko on the wall. It is very common to think that one knows that P for no other reason than that one sees, or otherwise senses, that P. Examples like this have encouraged some philosophers to examine the possibility that there is an external condition on knowledge, a causal condition in fact, which is missing in the Gettier examples. The idea would be, at its simplest, that I know that P if and only if my belief that P is caused by the state of affairs that makes P true. This condition seems to be satisfied when I believe there's a gecko on the wall because I can actually see one there, but not when the cause of my belief is that I was hypnotized.

This idea looks promising. It was felt that what prevented the Gettier examples counting as instances of knowledge was the fact that false propositions featured among the justifying grounds of Smith's beliefs. But a causal condition cannot fail to be true; if Smith believes that P, then whatever it is that causes him to believe that P must be the case. Moreover, a causal condition on knowledge would bind it to the world of objective realities; it could explain the feeling, which we first noted in connection with Plato, that a person with knowledge has somehow accessed objective realities while mere beliefs as such are inescapably subjective.

There are other reasons for thinking that the concept of knowledge may include a causal component. Take the case of the gecko again. We may at first be inclined to say that what makes the difference between my actually seeing a gecko on the wall and my mistakenly thinking that I am seeing a gecko on the wall is that in the first case there really is a gecko on the wall and in the second case there is not. But there can be cases where I mistakenly think I am seeing a gecko on the wall even though there really is a gecko on the wall. So this cannot be the whole story. Here is an example. There is a gecko on the wall, but interposed between it and me there is a holographic image of the gecko; this is what I see and the image is such that my visual experience is exactly as it would be if I were seeing the actual gecko. Here the difference between my seeing and my mistakenly thinking that I am seeing a gecko on the wall seems to be that in the one case there is a direct causal link between my visual experience and the presence of the gecko and in the other case there is not.

Memory provides another example. I seem to remember being swamped, at a young age, by a freak wave at the seaside. It is plausible to say that my memory is genuine – that is, I do remember *being swamped* – if and only if that actual event is a cause of the memory-impression I now have. Suppose that I forgot about it completely, but a hypnotist subsequently planted the thought of being swamped by a wave as a child in my mind. That's a false memory and what makes it false, it seems plausible to say, is that the causation is wrong.

It looks as if there might be a pattern here. It seems plausible to suggest there there is a causal condition on perceptual knowledge and also on memory knowledge, so why not in general on empirical knowledge at least? This idea may be reinforced by examples such as the following, adapted from Goldman (Goldman 1967). A travelling geologist observes a certain distribution of lava in the landscape and comes to believe that Mount Doom, which fills a large part of the southern horizon, suffered a volcanic eruption several thousand years ago. The distribution of the lava is an effect of that long-past eruption and the geologist reasons (correctly) that that is so. And now imagine the following variation. Mount Doom did erupt in the distant past and debris from that eruption was distributed around the landscape exactly as in the previous example. But now we are to imagine, additionally, that there was once a determined effort, by some mighty Titans perhaps, to tidy up the landscape by clearing away the debris. So everything was made smooth and easy on the eye. And then at some subsequent time, as tastes in landscape changed, it was felt the scene would look more exciting, more romantic, if it were made to appear that there had been an eruption; so a new generation of Titans replaced the debris pretty much as before. We now have a thrice changed landscape, changed once by the original eruption, once by the tidy Titans, and once by the romantic Titans, and this is the landscape that confronts our geologist. He reasons exactly as before. Here, however, it seems counter-intuitive to say that he knows. His conclusion happens to coincide with the facts: Mount Doom did erupt in the distant past and did spread lava about the landscape in the sort of pattern he sees. But the actual distribution of debris from which he reasons is artificial and not the direct effect of that eruption; the causal linkage has been disrupted. Many people find it natural to say that the geologist has knowledge where the landscape he sees is a direct effect of the eruption, but not where it has been changed. The suggestion now is that Gettier's examples fail to exemplify knowledge precisely because there is no *causal* connection between the fact which Smith believes obtains and his believing it, and it begins to look as if there might be serious mileage in the idea that knowledge is subject to a causal condition.

These examples are suggestive, but hardly decisive. For a start, the geologist's belief is the product of his inference, so the example lacks the pristine simplicity of the case where my belief that there is a gecko on the wall is a direct effect of the gecko's presence, mediated through my seeing it. But we could hardly exclude inference from among the antecedents of beliefs that are to count as knowledge, since this would rule out too many cases that we should want to include. In the first geological example given, we might present the chain connecting the eruption to the geologist's belief that an eruption occurred as follows:

Eruption → distribution of debris → G sees distribution of debris → G performs his inference → G believes there was an eruption

The idea is that this will count, for the purposes of the theory, as a knowledge-generating causal chain, because it includes a crucial causal link that is correctly reconstructed in the geologist's inference, even if the second pair of arrows do not themselves mark causal links. If we allow testimony to feature among the antecedents, as perhaps we should, then the chain will become more complicated. Suppose that Zoë believes (and putatively knows) that the cat is on the mat (P) because Alan has told her this. Here is one proposal as to how the appropriate causal connections might be presented, based, again, on an idea of Goldman's:

P → A believes that P → A asserts that P → Z believes A has asserted P → Z believes A believes P → Z believes P

But we shall have to add some ancillary chains that lock into this one: for example, Zoë's belief that Alan believes that P requires a belief in Alan's sincerity and her believing that P on the basis of Alan's sincerely held belief requires a belief in his competence to pronounce on the matter in question. In fact, this reconstruction of the causal antecedents of Zoë's belief is contentious. Hume, for example, who is often regarded as the supreme causal theorist of testimony, takes a very different view of her inferences; on his account, inferences to Alan's beliefs would not feature in the chain at all. We shall come to this later.

The causal theory of knowing has been thought to be problematic on other grounds. Some of the items that feature in the proposed causal chains – facts (e.g. that the gecko is on the wall) and states (e.g. my knowing or believing that the gecko is on the wall) – are thought to be of the wrong category to feature as either causes or effects. Events, it may be said, are what, *par excellence*, are fit to be causes and effects. But this is perhaps not too troublesome, because there will always be events that are connected with these facts or states. Some event – my spotting the gecko, for example – will inaugurate my state of believing that it is there, and some other event – its scurrying away – will terminate it.

It is, perhaps, harder to see how knowledge of general truths can be accommodated. I know that all men are mortal. But what might the causal antecedents of my belief that all men are mortal be, as required by the causal theory? Universal mortality is not itself an item in the causal order, so some special story will have to be spun about this item of common knowledge.

Finally, consider knowledge of some future event: the next solar eclipse, say. It will generally be granted that I can know that this is going to take place on whatever the date may be, long before it happens. But how could an event still lying in the future *cause* a current state of affairs – my believing there is going to be an eclipse? Causes don't, so it is usually thought, work backwards. One rather heroic approach here might be to deny that this is an example of knowledge at all. For all I know, it might be said, some massive catastrophe could overwhelm the solar system before the eclipse happens. Some people have indeed held, for reasons like this, that all future events necessarily lie outside the domain of possible knowledge:

> If "figs never grow on thistles" is taken to mean "None ever have and none ever will", then it is implied that I *know* that none ever have, but only that I *believe* that none ever will.
>
> (Austin 1961: 69)

The thought behind this is that the past is closed, secure from the vagaries of chance and change in the course of nature, but the future is open; anything *might* happen. Consequently, although one can, perhaps, know what has happened, one cannot know what *will* happen. If this argument is to be effective in distinguishing between knowledge of the past and "knowledge" of the future, it must be understood as turning on something other than sceptical considerations, since those would apply equally to the past. As Russell hypothesized, the world might have come into existence five minutes ago complete with all my "memories", in which case everything I now take myself to know about a past more remote than five minutes ago will fail to be knowledge. The interesting argument has to turn on a point about the metaphysics of time – that the future *really is* open – so that propositions about the future cannot be assigned a definite truth-value.

It would take us a long way off course to pursue this matter further. Let us notice, though, that the denial that we can have knowledge of the future is at odds with our ordinary ways of thinking about knowledge and about the future. If someone asks me whether I'm busy tomorrow afternoon, they want to know whether I shall be busy, and my answer will purport to deliver what they want, namely, knowledge; that is the nature of questions and answers. I might, of course, on some particular occasion, reply truthfully that I don't know; but it would be ridiculously eccentric to reply in that way on a regular basis to no matter what question about my future. I frequently have (intentional) knowledge of what I am going to do. Here perhaps the committed causal theorist can make headway by invoking the idea of a common cause. The very same thing that causes my belief is also a cause of whatever it is I believe. The intention that will cause my activity tomorrow afternoon is a cause of my now having the belief I have about that activity. The ongoing chain of astronomical events that will issue in the coming eclipse also feeds the astronomers' predictions of the eclipse, which in turn generate my belief. And in all such cases, the belief I end up with counts as knowledge. And so on.

But it would be a mistake to get hung up on the strategies for handling the harder cases before we are satisfied that the causal theory actually holds the answer to our problems about the nature of knowledge. There are strong reasons for thinking it doesn't. Consider this elaboration of the Mount Doom example, originally due to Dretske (Dretske 1971). This time the southern horizon is occupied by two mountains, Doom and Gloom. Our geologist reasons as before, correctly reconstructing in his mind the chain of events that link this spread of volcanic debris with the eruption of Doom, and, in this case, there has been no Titanic intervention. But the fact of the matter is that an eruption of Mount Gloom would have produced pretty much the same observable result. In these circumstances we shall demand more of our geologist than that in his reasoning he reconstructs the actual causal history correctly. If he neglects to consider and then to eliminate the possibility that it was an eruption of Gloom that produced the evidence with which he is presented, I doubt we shall allow him knowledge. For all he knows, in that case, it might have been Gloom that erupted. It is only an accident that he happened to get it right. And it seems counter-intuitive to suppose that in these circumstances he *knows* Doom produced this spread of debris.

Tracking the truth

The moral of this story is that the causal condition, even if it is necessary, is not strong enough to complete our analysis of the conditions on knowledge. Our geologist is clearly terribly unreliable. His reasoning is seriously defective. Even though it correctly reconstructs the actual chain of causes, how could it possibly produce knowledge when it is corrupted by negligence? This suggests we might make more headway by exploring the idea of reliability.

The reasoning used by our geologist cannot be relied on to deliver the truth, because, in the event that Mount Gloom, not Mount Doom, had erupted, he would still have used the reasoning he did and come to the same conclusion (wrong, on this hypothesis). Since his method of reasoning doesn't, in the circumstances, exclude that wrong conclusion, it is unreliable. We can't trust it to deliver the truth. What we want, it seems, is a result in which not only does he believe that Mount Gloom erupted, since it did, but also he would not not believe that Mount Gloom had erupted, if it had not (and, say, Doom had instead). More generally, we want him to have used a belief-getting method that, in the sort of circumstances in which he finds himself, will get him to believe that P if P is true and not to believe that P if P is false. If he satisfies those conditions his belief "tracks the truth", to use a phrase invented by Robert Nozick (Nozick 1981: 172–8). And the idea we are now considering is that there is a tracking requirement on knowledge. Alternatively, since the tracking requirement is expressed through conditionals, we are considering what is sometimes called the conditional analysis of knowledge.

The devil is, as ever, in the detail. Consider the following (possibly real-life) example. It is quite like the case of our careless geologist, but differs in one extremely important respect. It is said that Prince Potemkin, when Governor of the freshly annexed Crimea, built a series of village façades along the route he was to take with his mistress, the Empress of Russia, Catherine the Great, on her progress through her new territory. So we can imagine the Empress, as she rides by, gazing with admiration at the visible front of what seems to be a village, a very model of neatness and rural busyness. As it happens, it is a real village. But does Catherine *know* that it is? Certainly she *believes* that it is, and her belief satisfies the causal condition on knowledge, although we have found reason to think that that in itself is too weak; still, her belief that there is a village yonder is certainly caused by the actual village she is gazing at. We cannot say, however, that in the circumstances contrived by Potemkin, she would not now believe there was a village in view if there were not. She would believe it even if she were gazing at a Potemkin fake. So her belief doesn't satisfy the tracking condition. In the peculiar circumstances of the case, the method by which she came to believe there was a village yonder was not reliable. So perhaps we shall judge that she doesn't know she is looking at a village.

So the argument goes, but it doesn't seem perfectly obvious to me. Certainly it was a lucky chance that, in the peculiar environment she was in, she was right. But the method she used, viewing the passing scene, is one that can be relied on to deliver the truth in *normal* circumstances. So someone might argue as follows. "Given Potemkin's tricks, it was luck that Catherine got it right. But her belief was right. And that it was right was attributable to the fact that it was caused by the circumstance that made it true. It was not just a subjective impression that she had, but a belief standing in an objective relation with that aspect of the real world of which it was a representation. It would be outrageous to deny that this amounted to knowledge, while admitting, as we surely must, that she would have had knowledge in an exactly similar situation if Potemkin hadn't built his fakes. How could this wholly extraneous fact make any difference to her present state and her present relationship to the facts?"

Some people may be convinced by this. Provided Catherine uses a method that is reliable in all normal circumstances, it may be said, we should allow her knowledge; and everything is normal in the *immediate* circumstances in which she finds herself. Notice the difference between her and the geologist. The geologist was negligent. Mount Gloom was an obvious candidate for being the cause of the distribution of lava, and he should have eliminated it before attributing the spread of lava to an eruption of Doom. Catherine, however, was not negligent; she reacted as any normal rational human being would. It would, of course, be different if she had known about, or even if she had had reason to suspect, Potemkin's tricks. If we add that into the story, I daresay everyone will feel that she didn't know; a person with that information will surely have to have excluded trickery before we allow them knowledge.

Other people will not be satisfied. They will say that even though we couldn't sensibly demand more of Catherine, it is still just good luck in the circumstances that she was right on this occasion. The normally reliable method for coming by information about villages cannot be relied on to deliver the truth in Potemkin country and Catherine *is* in Potemkin country; it's pure chance that when she used the normally reliable method here it worked. In this country she needs to use a Potemkin-proof method.

The crisis in epistemology

The conditional analysis is currently the chief focus of attention within the broad tradition of philosophizing about knowledge that has been dominant for the past thirty or forty years, that is, the tradition that seeks to analyse the concept of knowledge in terms of an individual's beliefs. There is no doubt that it goes some way towards answering Meno's Challenge. It seems pretty clear that if P is true and I believe it, I would still prefer it to be the case, at least once I think about the alternatives, that I would not believe it if P were not true and would believe it if P were true (as, *ex hypothesi*, it is). Otherwise, scepticism threatens. Tracking is good. But there are at least three points to be made.

First, this type of analysis doesn't give us some kind of easy algorithm that enables us to determine when a person does or doesn't know that P. My intuitions about Catherine the Great, for example, when she is in Potemkin land, are not clear. I still don't know what to say about her, in the situation described.

Secondly, the tracking idea provides neither specific rules, nor even a general method, for obtaining knowledge. It explains, or at least it purports to explain, the conditions under which a person's belief may be said to amount to knowledge, but it doesn't provide directions for achieving that state. It specifies a state that withstands sceptical challenge, but doesn't tell us how to get there. This is not necessarily a disadvantage. Perhaps it is a mistake to look for just one standard type of recipe for attaining knowledge. Still, this is a point that distinguishes the tracking theory from some others we have considered. A causal theorist, for example, has a clear general idea about how a state must come into being if it is to count as one of knowing that P; it has to have been caused in a way that connects the knower's psychological state to the state of affairs she knows about, even if there is some debate about what kinds of links in the chain are permissible. Similarly, a justificationist holds that the knower's belief must be adequately supported by reasons. The tracking theorist, on the other hand, can be open-minded about how the belief that qualifies as knowledge is reached, provided only that the method is reliable in the sense specified by the conditional analysis.

Finally, although we can all perhaps agree that it is good to have true beliefs that, somehow or other, track truth, it doesn't actually *follow* that such beliefs amount to knowledge. Meno was, no doubt, right to suggest that knowledge is more highly valued than (mere) true belief and right to demand that we explain why. But it would be a fallacy to argue that any true belief that has some feature, like tracking, that makes it better than mere (and perhaps accidentally) true belief must on that account *be* knowledge. When we were reviewing some of Plato's thoughts in Chapter 1, we noted several aspects of the concept of knowledge which a good account of the concept might be expected to recognize. The tracking analysis as such has nothing to say about any of these. And, in fact, the whole tradition of epistemic individualism, originating in Descartes's anxieties about scepticism and his distaste for traditional book-learning, is silent about them.

Let us recall what they were, in no particular order. First, a good account of knowledge should help us to see why knowledge rather than belief seems, if our ordinary ways of speaking are any guide, to be the proper object of enquiry; why it is that, when people make enquiries seriously, it is not only natural but more or less inevitable that we should describe them as wanting to know something, as seeking knowledge on some matter. Closely connected with this point, we want an account of knowledge that will help us understand why the word *know* happily tolerates interrogative constructions when the word *believe* does not. It makes, on any view, a striking contrast between the two vocabularies and it seems plausible to say that this grammatical property will be an essential feature of any verb that is capable of expressing the aim of someone making an enquiry from a position of ignorance. The enquirer asks where the railway station is because she wants to *know* where it is; it makes no sense to describe her as wanting to *believe* where it is. Finally, and still connected with the previous points, it appeared that the idea of knowledge was connected with notions of expertise, authority and teaching; experts, speaking with authority, can, under certain conditions, so we often think, engender knowledge in their audience. The tradition of individualistic analysis is largely inimical to these notions. It is possible that the special feature of tracking fits into this ensemble of properties, that it is, so to speak, a proper part of a package which includes these other features, but in that case it remains to show that it is. In any event, it seems unlikely that tracking is a completely self-standing property, which alone makes all the difference between knowing and believing.

Now, although many recent philosophers of knowledge seem to have been mesmerized by the thought that their overriding task is to provide, at all costs, an analysis of the psychological state of the individual knower by listing the necessary and sufficient conditions for their knowing that P, other philosophers have begun to find this perception of their task unsatisfactory. Decades of unremitting work have signally failed to yield an account along these lines that commands general assent or that manages to respond to all our questions about knowledge. So it has come to seem to some philosophers that epistemology itself has reached a crisis point. It is as if the very project itself has degenerated into nothing more than a kind of contest to see who is cleverest at inventing ever more bizarre counter-examples or adding yet new twists to already mind-bogglingly elaborate accounts of what it is for an individual to know that P. (See Kaplan 1985 for one eloquent protest.) Perhaps we have managed to convey some of this flavour, although we have avoided the more tortuous and exotic analyses of knowledge to be found in the literature. (Readers interested in savouring more advanced examples of the genre will find some of them listed in the Guide to Further Reading.) It is, as we noted earlier, all rather reminiscent of Ptolemaic astronomy; as if the point were to preserve the broad scheme of this style of analysis, at no matter what cost in terms of *ad hoc* complexifications, dreamt up to cover new observations (new counter-examples).

So it is perhaps not surprising that some contemporary philosophers (Kaplan, for one instance), thinking along these lines, should have given up completely on the idea of analysing knowledge and settled for a different conception of the goals of epistemology, such as those described in the Introduction. The idea then is: forget about knowledge; come clean; focus explicitly on the question of how to get the best quality beliefs. True beliefs are plainly of interest to us, since we need them to guide us successfully in the conduct of our lives; and from this point of view, as Meno pointed out, knowledge confers no further benefit on us. So it behoves us to think how true beliefs are to be obtained, and in general how we may maximize the chances of our beliefs' being true. The various attempts to complete the third clause of a tripartite analysis, or to find some adequate augmentation of the analysis, seek in their several ways to guarantee or otherwise satisfy us that whatever belief is in question is indeed true. But to think of the task of completing or supplementing the third clause as a matter of perfecting a definition of *knowledge*, answerable to our intuitions about what should and should not be honoured with this title, forces us into a Procrustean bed that only distorts the enquiry and limits its scope, not least when it is assumed that there is a single essence of knowledge, which a good analysis will capture.

There is, however, a different kind of approach that might be tried in the face of the crisis. In a way it is more conservative than the one described above, but in another way more radical. It is conservative in that it retains the traditional focus on the idea of *knowledge*, seeking an understanding of that concept; it is radical in the way it aims to achieve this understanding. It doesn't look for an *analysis* of the concept in the traditional manner originated by Plato. Rather, it tries to understand the concept by examining the role that it plays in our lives and its place in the general economy of our concepts. What does it do for us? How should we fare without it? This is the approach which I favour and which I shall develop in the chapters that follow. I maintain that the concept of knowledge matters to us. It is extremely important. We could not do without it. The problem is to understand why it matters, why it is important.

The idea of public knowledge

How, then, does the concept of knowledge feature in our lives? What uses do we put it to? One thing that may strike us immediately, when we ask such questions, is that knowledge, as we often conceive of it, has a public aspect, an aspect that is liable to be missed entirely when we focus on the task of delivering an analysis of the conditions for some individual's knowing that P. Consider the uses of the noun *knowledge*. We often use it to refer to what we seem to think of as a kind of public commodity, something that may be available to anyone; we have already noticed how encyclo-paedias, for example, aim to collect items of human knowledge together in a readily accessible format so that anyone may access them. The same idea is enshrined in those PhD rubrics that require that a dissertation should make a significant contribution to knowledge. Again, it occurs when London cab drivers apply themselves to the task of learning what they call "The Knowledge", or when we speak of matters of common knowledge. And, as we saw in Chapter 1, this way of thinking is manifest in the use Greeks had for a plural of their word for knowledge; for them, not only is there such a thing as human knowledge considered generally, but there are also separate "knowledges" (branches of knowledge), like cooking and astronomy, all capable of being taught by a master to his pupils. As with the Greek word, so with our own word *science*, taken from the Latin for knowledge and meaning, according to one dictionary definition, "a body of knowledge organized in a systematic manner". That definition captures pretty well the idea of what students, learning the various sciences, ideally want to master: a body of established and publicly available knowledge. These examples all invoke the notion of what Karl Popper (1902–94) called objective knowledge and opposed to knowledge in a subjective sense. The latter is the dominant concern of the kinds of theorists whose work we considered in Chapter 3, for whom Popper disparagingly coined the term "belief-theorists". Popper's view of what objective knowledge comprises ("problems, theories, and arguments as such") is, perhaps, rather idiosyncratic (Popper 1973: 109). But, the Popperian idea that libraries (or, come to that, encyclopaedias, dictionaries and so on) are, among other things, repositories of knowledge seems unproblematic. Even the verb *know*, which is typically used to ascribe a state of mind to individuals, may also be used impersonally to indicate that some bit of knowledge is the common property of several individuals: "it is well known (widely known) that . . . ".

It doesn't take much reflection to realize, once the idea of knowledge having a public aspect is brought into focus, that we actually live in an environment that is saturated with knowledge, or at least what we take to be knowledge, available to us but also external to us. We can easily have recourse to encyclopaedias, libraries and the web, to search out particular bits of knowledge that we may want, or else trawl these resources on the off chance that we may get to know something new and interesting. In our literate and technologically proficient culture it is, in fact, vastly easier to get knowledge on a huge variety of topics than it was for even our quite recent ancestors. Nowadays there is more knowledge about, and it is much more easily obtained. But it is even more noteworthy that much of the knowledge that is available to us is, so to speak, thrust upon us; we don't have to go out of our way to find it, it is all about us, like the air we breathe, unavoidable, and, in the urban West at least, essential for our kind of life. Think of the labels on goods in the shops, the names on the spines of books, inscriptions on buildings such as offices, libraries and churches, signposts, advertisements, public notices, street signs, number plates on cars, and so on; all of them are designed to convey knowledge to the public at large, or at any rate to anyone who may be interested in acquiring the sort of knowledge in question, and all are bearers of information that anyone who reads may acquire, information that may be useful and even necessary for us to have. As I have walked along the streets near my house, I have both got to know and frequently been reminded, because I can see and read, that here is Sainsbury's, there is WHSmith's, there's the library and here's the Police Station, that is Wellington Park, this is a one-way street with restricted parking, and *Measure for Measure* is playing at The Old Tobacco Factory. What goes for me, surely, goes for nearly everybody who lives in the same vicinity. Someone may say, "This is information, and, to be sure, there is lots of information about; but it doesn't deserve to be called *knowledge*". But why doesn't it? The point is, in every case, to let people *know* something. Where does the idea come from that knowledge, as well as being valuable or useful, should also be hard to get?

There is a further point. It would be entirely wrong to picture this situation, in the way encouraged perhaps by belief-theorists, as one in which each of us, being individually bombarded with information, carries round her own personal packet, securely insulated from her fellow beings. Of course, there is no way I could divine exactly what my neighbour has registered in our environment or what she has retained out of all the multifarious items of knowledge to which we have both been exposed. But it is safe for me to assume that she will have registered and retained a good deal of it. We can both assume that we share a substantial amount of knowledge about the locality we inhabit and about the larger world; moreover, we can assume that each of us, if it proves necessary for a given purpose, may be in a position to supply deficits in the other's knowledge. It would be impossible to exaggerate the importance of assumptions like these. They are essential lubricants of our kind of life; it's important that we know pretty well what knowledge we can take for granted in those with whom we have dealings and what we can't. There are many situations in which it is helpful, even essential, that I should know that you know that P, and even that you should know that I know that you know that P. For some collaborative activities, perhaps we can go even further; perhaps it may matter that I should know that you know that I know that you know that P and vice versa. Think of such things as rock-climbing, dancing, playing in a quartet. What is at issue here is not merely knowledge that is public, in the sense that two or more people may know exactly the same thing. Rather, we are considering situations in which more or less complicated structures involving mutual recognition of knowledge in each other are realized. In such cases, let us say there is *mutual* knowledge that P. It is very important, given our kind of life, that our concept of knowledge supports both these ideas: public knowledge and mutual knowledge.

Again, to narrow the focus to something rather specialized but nonetheless important to us all, consider the practice of science. Clearly, a scientist, working at the cutting edge of her subject and writing up the results of her research, will not normally begin right at the bottom; she will assume, as she is surely entitled to assume, that some things are common knowledge within the community she is addressing. Members of the scientific community can rely on their fellows knowing the basics. Scientific papers would be extremely tedious if they could not. But there is more to it than this. Recently philosophers have begun to notice that reliance on knowledge gained by other people has an important role in the scientific enterprise itself. John Hardwig, for example, has commented illuminatingly on the fact that there are some multi-authored scientific papers such that the experimental work that feeds into them literally could not be accomplished by a single individual in a human lifetime (Hardwig 1991). In this sense, some advanced scientific research is necessarily collaborative. Hardwig's central point is that scientists have to trust one another, and in what follows I shall have more to say about the role of trust in the business of knowledge; it is crucial. The point I want to make here, however, is that some knowledge, far from being the prized achievement of a solitary intellect, as conceived according to the Cartesian ideal, is itself the product of an essentially collaborative enterprise; to which we may add that success in such enterprises may often require that there be mutual knowledge among the collaborators.

Of course, much of what has been said here about science will also go for other knowledge-orientated pursuits. Consider history, for another example. Some historical results are obtained at junctures where radically different disciplines converge. Such results may require contributions from people with quite disparate skills and expertise, which it would be hard, if not impossible, for any one individual to combine. Thus, the evaluation of archaeological finds, statistical analysis, expert interpretation of inscriptions, judicious evaluation of written records and so on may all in different ways contribute to the overall picture that a certain sort of historian finally presents. The different elements in the picture may, perhaps, be drawn together by a single person, but it is hardly possible she should have discovered each of the elements, Crusoe-wise, by her own unaided effort; she has to take things on trust from others.

The importance of testimony

Observations like these inevitably prompt questions as to how knowledge is made available to other people, and how mutual knowledge arises. Perhaps shared experience plays a part: together we observe that the straight stick, on being partially immersed in water, presents a crooked appearance and perhaps we take it that our co-observers, being human like ourselves, have registered the same phenomenon and also made the same assumption about us. But if this is part of the story, it is, surely, only a tiny part. What really matters is that we have evolved a language that enables us to communicate facts to one another. We have developed ways of representing facts symbolically and in a manner that is intelligible within a given linguistic community. The upshot is that we can communicate what we know to one another by means of language and, because we are self-conscious and observant communicators, structures of mutual knowledge can arise. We can talk and write to and for one another, in the confident expectation that what we say and write will be understood. Written and spoken utterances may serve many different purposes; but conspicuous among them is the fact that they are the means by which vast amounts of what we think of as knowledge is communicated, accessed and shared. In the rest of this book, we are going to be largely concerned with this use of language. We shall find that it is very revealing about the nature of knowledge.

Let us begin with written utterances. These are often, in effect, publicly accessible repositories of what, by their means, can become public knowledge; written records, inscriptions and the like can be observed by any number of people, who, in observing and understanding them for what they are, obtain the knowledge they embody. Such records range from the trivial and ephemeral (the label on a can of beans) to the more or less permanent (inscriptions on monuments or public buildings). They include an enormous diversity of types of item, such as the daily newspaper, the standing orders of institutions, institutional archives, books of history, reports of scientific experiments, and so on. The information they contain is, as often as not, completely encoded in propositional form, but this is not always so. Think of maps. If I want to know the way from Bristol to Nempnett Thrubwell, I will do better to look at a map than read a text or try to take the directions on board aurally. And, of course, in saying that these vehicles of knowledge are themselves public I am not overlooking the fact that access to them, and hence to the knowledge that they contain, may be restricted. They are public in the sense that, in principle, they can be observed by more than one person, any of whom, if they understand them, may thereby acquire the knowledge they contain. That doesn't mean to say that the knowledge may not sometimes be kept secret. But the very idea of keeping something secret implies the possibility of revealing it; if knowledge were not naturally communicable, there could be no secrets and no ethical problems about privacy, freedom of information and so on.

Oral communication, no doubt, came first in the order of things, but it is, above all, the ability to embody knowledge in bits of writing and other enduring symbols, like maps, charts and graphs, that marks our kind of civilization, and makes us the kind of civilized creatures that we are.

Telling someone what's what, whether orally or in writing, is what philosophers call "testimony". This is high-sounding language for something common and familiar. When I told my wife this morning that it was raining, that was testimony. By telling her, I let her know (as I thought) that it was raining. This is an instance of testimony in its most elementary form; telling is the most basic testimonial act in our repertoire, and in the discussions that follow we shall take it as representative of the whole family of testimonial speech-acts. But we should note that there are other members of the family: announcing, reporting, notifying, declaring and stating, for example. What warrants grouping all these together is this: when there is no deceit, the intention of a speaker performing any of these speech-acts will be to convey knowledge to an audience, to let them know something; and when all goes well she will succeed. They are, therefore, quite different from other speech-acts performed by uttering sentences in the indicative mood, such as voicing opinions, hazarding guesses and speculating.

Now, the trouble with accounts of knowledge which, like the belief-theoretical accounts we have looked at, treat it as a purely subjective phenomenon, is that it is very hard to see how knowledge, so conceived, is communicated at all: that is, how a hearer can get to *know* that P from hearing someone produce a certain type of utterance whose content is P. It is, perhaps, even harder to see how there could be public and mutual knowledge under such a conception. Belief-theoretical conceptions of knowledge are not well adapted to explaining these structures. But the possibility of communicating knowledge by say-so to other people and thereby creating structures of mutual knowledge is deeply embedded in our ordinary ways of thinking and behaving. When I tell my wife that I have told you that the key is under the doormat, it is so that she may know that you know where it is; that will set her mind at rest. And I take it that you know where it is for no other reason than that I *have* told you. This way of thinking is classically captured in Hilaire Belloc's cautionary tale:

> You know – at least you *ought* to know,
> For I have often told you so –
> That Children never are allowed
> To leave their Nurses in a Crowd.
>
> > ("Jim, who ran away from his nurse
> > and was eaten by a lion" in *Cautionary Tales*)

Outside the philosophical classroom, we take it as a *given* that knowledge can and does get transmitted through telling. Amazingly, there are philosophers who would deny it: such is the power of an entrenched tradition. Thus Jonathan Barnes, referring to some common-sense remarks of Myles Burnyeat:

> He means that if x knows that p and x says to y that p, then (normally) y thereby comes to know that p. Now I think that that is quite false – it is a lot harder to acquire knowledge than Burnyeat imagines. No doubt we all do pick up beliefs in that second hand fashion, and I fear that we often suppose that such scavenging yields knowledge. But that is only a sign of our colossal credulity; the method Burnyeat describes is a rotten way of acquiring beliefs, and it is no way at all of acquiring knowledge.   (Barnes 1980: 200)

This blanket condemnation of testimony-based beliefs and testimony-based knowledge is typical of the individualistic philosophical culture inspired by Descartes's general disparagement of textbook learning, tradition and authority. But how can it possibly be justified? In Chapter 3, I asked where modern analytical philosophers of knowledge got their intuitions about knowledge from (p. 41). A plausible answer seemed to be that, no longer supposing they can access a Platonic world of pure ideas, they must draw on their ordinary linguistic know-how for their analyses. But our ordinary ways of thinking and speaking do not warrant Barnes's strictures. So where do *his* intuitions come from? Are we to suppose that, after all, he has gained an insight into some transcendent Platonic idea?

In the following chapters, I am going to consider knowledge in its public aspect. How exactly can a bit of knowledge be made available in written records or through ordinary say-so? What is the mechanism? And what does this reveal about the nature of knowledge? Knowledge isn't *really* like a commodity, a concrete item that can literally be passed from one person to another. And, in any case, when a person conveys a bit of knowledge to me, she doesn't thereby lose possession of it herself. For this reason, I have sometimes spoken of knowledge as being "commonable", hoping by this coinage to capture this peculiar feature of the concept.

There is, undoubtedly, a kind of puritanical notion abroad that knowledge ought to be difficult, a prize that can only be won by serious individual effort; hence Barnes's remarks. And it may well be that the original acquisition of some bits of knowledge is hard and that special intellectual gifts are required to comprehend some truths. As it seems to me, these are points about (some of) the objects of knowledge. In what follows I hope to convince the reader that they are not truths about knowledge *as such*.

Learning from testimony

Preamble

Not all philosophers have taken Barnes's uncompromising stand. In recent years especially, they have increasingly come to recognize that testimony is, for each of us, an extremely important source of beliefs, and quite a number have recognized that it is often seen as a source of knowledge and have therefore tried to work out how this might be possible. These are the matters we are now going to investigate. Even philosophers who have given up on the project of achieving a satisfactory analysis of knowledge, and who have, on that account, focused on the question how to improve the quality of our beliefs, should be interested in the workings of testimony, since clearly so many of our beliefs are attributable to it; such philosophers may want to examine the conditions (supposing, *pace* Barnes, that there are some) under which beliefs obtained from testimony can satisfy proper standards of quality. For my part, I think that a correct understanding of how testimony works will give us the clue we need to discover the real nature of knowledge.

How, then, do we learn from testimony? How does testimony engender beliefs in its hearers? Under what circumstances might it engender knowledge? Above all, what does knowledge have to be like if it is to be obtained by these means? In this chapter, I shall discuss some of the larger issues that any philosopher asking these questions has to confront, chiefly through an examination of a long-standing controversy. This concerns the question how, in the first place, a person acquires the testimonial method of coming by beliefs, or, as it may be, of obtaining knowledge. It is important that that question is distinguished from another with which it is apt to be confused: how does a person come by this or that particular belief or particular bit of knowledge using the method of testimony?

Generally speaking, theories in the field of testimony have been subordinate to other theories. Philosophers who have developed them have mostly done so with the aim of fitting them into a wider scheme of things to which they are already committed. Perhaps they already have fairly fixed ideas about the sort of thing that knowledge is, and seek to explain how it can be obtained through testimony in a way that can be made consistent with their preconceptions. Or, as is the case with Hume, as we shall shortly see, they are strongly committed to a general theory about how beliefs concerning matters that the subject is not currently able to observe for herself can be obtained, and feel constrained to make the testimonial route conform to this independently conceived theory. I claim for the theory that I am going to put forward that it is not subordinate in this sense. On the contrary, I think that by unfolding, *ab initio*, the mechanism of testimony, we can obtain a genuinely new insight into the nature of knowledge. But that is for later.

A Humean approach

Now for the controversy just mentioned. Hume is one main protagonist. He, more perhaps than any other philosopher in the philosophical canon, recognized the extraordinary importance of testimony in the lives of human beings:

> There is no species of reasoning more common, more useful, and even necessary to human life, than that which is derived from the testimony of men, and the reports of eye-witnesses and spectators. (Hume 1975: 111)

Sadly, his discussion of this "species of reasoning" is often held to be outstandingly bad and is compared unfavourably with that of his contemporary and critic, Thomas Reid, the other protagonist in the debate. I think Hume is widely misunderstood on this topic and is actually a lot closer to Reid than is generally realized. I also think that Hume's account, as far as it goes, is on the right track.

First, some preliminary points. Hume regularly describes the process we are concerned with in terms of the hearer getting to *believe* that P from a speaker's testimony. This is because he writes in the tradition we described in Chapter 1, according to which you can only know truths whose self-evidence or demonstrability you appreciate. But nothing you believe *on testimony* do you believe *because* it is self-evident or demonstrable (which it very likely isn't), so your testimony-born belief will not be eligible, in Hume's idiolect, to be called knowledge. All that matters for our present purposes, however, is that the hearer ends up with a certain thought, P, which she takes to represent how things actually are. *Pace* Hume, in the vernacular, when things go well, we call this knowledge, and I think that *knowledge* is the proper word for it (when things have gone well). But, in any case, it would be wrong to get hung up on Hume's preference for *belief*, since at this stage nothing turns on which word we use.

The second preliminary point is this. Hume standardly uses the word *inference* for the hearer's passage of mind from her hearing a testimony to her consequent belief. To our ears this suggests conscious reasoning from evidence to a conclusion. But for Hume any rule-governed passage of mind from some sort of sensory input to a belief is an inference. It need not be conscious and it may be pretty much automatic. He would be happy to say that Pavlov's dogs inferred that food was on its way when they heard the bell. (In fact he would be happy, in spite of recognizing that what they do is the result of conditioning, to say they reach their conclusion through *reasoning* (see Hume 1978: I, iii, 16).) We need to be careful not to read too much into Hume's terminology; I think, perhaps, some commentators have.

Finally, we are not concerned with any old case where a listener ends up believing (knowing) something on the basis of being told something. We are not concerned with the sort of case where you tell me that the train is running 50 minutes late and I infer (Hume's sense) that you are a Glaswegian. This is not what we might call "testimonial inference". It fails on two counts. First, I should most probably have formed the same belief *whatever* you had said. What triggered my conclusion was the accent in which you spoke, not the content of your utterance and not the nature of the speech-act you performed, neither of which I may even have properly appreciated.

In a testimonial inference, however, it matters that the trigger is perceived *as* testimony – a telling, a reporting, an announcing or similar informative speech-act – and, in a testimonial inference, the content of the belief with which I end up must be identical with, or equivalent to, the content of the testimonial utterance. I must have obtained my belief through recognizing that content as the content of a bit of testimony. You tell me *that the train is late*, and, recognizing that you are *telling* me this and that *this* is what you are telling me, I come to believe (or, as many of us would cheerfully say, I get to know) *that the train is late*. In virtue of the hearer's understanding the speech-act as testimony, the content of the speaker's utterance is, in favourable circumstances, *preserved* in the hearer's subsequent cognitive state; where the speaker has told the hearer that P, the hearer ends up believing (knowing) that P. (This idea of content preservation in the context of testimony is due to Burge (1993). More of it later.)

Now to serious business. Hume's general pronouncements about testimonial inference are of this sort:

> our assurance in any argument of this kind is derived from no other principle than our observation of the veracity of human testimony, and of the usual conformity of facts to the reports of witnesses. It being a general maxim, that no objects have any discoverable connection together, and that all the inferences, which we can draw from one to another, are founded merely on our experience of their constant and regular conjunction; it is evident, that we ought not to make an exception to this maxim in favour of human testimony, whose connexion with any event seems, in itself, as little necessary as any other.
>
> (1975: X.i, 111)

Or, again, a little later:

> The reason, why we place any credit in witnesses and historians, is not derived from any connexion, which we perceive *a priori*, between testimony and reality, but because we are accustomed to find a conformity between them . . .
>
> (1975: X.i, 112)

Remarks like these are an affirmation that testimonial inferences are subject to what in the first *Enquiry* he calls "that great guide of human life" (1975: IV.ii, 36), namely, *Experience*. In other words, there is no reason independent of experience, no a priori reason, to connect testimonial utterances with states of affairs. Rather we get to believe something via a testimonial inference ultimately because experience has habituated us to associate one thing with another thing. The formation of testimony-born beliefs fits into the general scheme of Hume's empiricist philosophy, according to which, for example, on seeing a fire I get to believe that I shall be warmed; my previous experience of regular conjunctions of fire and feelings of warmth has habituated me to associate the two. Hume's idea is that habitual association will also explain why I believe things on testimony.

How does this work out in detail? When I perform a testimonial inference, precisely what have I learnt to associate with what? One possibility might be this. I hear you say "There's a fire!" and I thereupon begin to believe that there's a fire for no other reason than that experience has led me to associate utterances of that sentence with there being fire; in just the same way I might conclude that there's a fire on seeing smoke. Or, to take another example, Pooh hears Rabbit utter the sentence "There's honey for tea", and thereupon believes that there's honey for tea because experience has led him to associate utterances of that sentence with there being honey for tea. In the same way, when Pooh sees the bees he comes to believe that there is honey to be had since he has learnt from experience to associate bees with honey: bees mean honey. These examples come from D. H. Mellor, who says:

> In both cases *what really matters* is the same: that the sign he observes directly – the bees, Rabbit's saying "[there's honey for tea]" – should be correlated with honey.
>
> (Mellor 1990: 88, emphasis added)

I think a number of Hume's readers have supposed that he sub-scribes to a theory about how we come to make the testimonial inferences we do along these lines, that this is how the association-ist theory of belief-formation applies to testimony-engendered beliefs. There are compelling reasons for thinking that this theory cannot be correct, and, as far as I can see, no good reasons for thinking it is Hume's theory. In the first place, it is wrong to suppose that the way we acquire beliefs from testimony is through hearing utterances of particular *given* sentences that in our experience have turned out to be correlated with particular facts. The idea would be that in such cases we acquire our belief only because experience has taught us to associate "There's honey for tea" with there being honey for tea, "The cat is on the mat" with the cat's being on the mat, "It's pouring with rain" with its raining, and so on. But this cannot be right. On this view we could never acquire beliefs from utterances of hitherto unheard sentences. We can, and we do. Any plausible theory of testimony must accommodate this fundamental point. As readers of James Thurber will appreciate, it had to be *possible* for the man's wife to learn from his totally unprecedented say-so that there really was a unicorn in the garden which ate a lily, or the fable would have had no moral. (When he told her this, she called a psychiatrist. And when she told the psychiatrist that her husband had reported the presence of a lily-eating unicorn in the garden, he certified her mad (Thurber 1954: 230–31).)

Secondly, it would be absurd, in any case, to think that (mere) *utterances* of particular sentences are, as such, correlated in the appropriate way with the facts. The correlation, if there is one, has to be with utterances of a particular kind, a certain class of speech-acts, tellings, reportings and so on; they have to be *testimonial* utterances. Thus when Mellor says that Rabbit's saying "There is honey for tea" is correlated with honey, we need to understand the sense in which Rabbit *says* this in a special way. Rabbit is *telling* Pooh that there is honey for tea. There are other possibilities: for example, he could utter the selfsame sentence interrogatively, in order to *ask* whether there is honey for tea; or it might be embedded in a conditional – "If there is honey for tea, I'm definitely staying"; again, he might be a philosophical rabbit, producing the sentence only to make a point.

Hume was certainly aware of the essential role played by the speech-act *as such* in testimonial inferences; thus, he clearly recognizes that different audiences might actually hear one and the same sentence, or string of sentences, differently, as being instances of different kinds of speech-act, when he writes:

[margin handwritten note: where did we get these ideas]

> If one person sits down to read a book as a romance, and another as a true history, they plainly receive the same ideas, and in the same order; nor does the incredulity of the one, and the belief of the other, hinder them from putting the very same sense upon their author. (Hume 1978: I, iii, vii, 97–8)

Here the sense of what is said is the same; but the speech-acts, as perceived by these different readers, are different and consequently their responses are different; one believes what she reads and the other does not.

It seems that an empiricist who wants to maintain her central doctrine will have to improve on the crude associationist account just sketched. She must somehow accommodate the possibility of learning from testimonial acts that are constituted by utterances of quite unfamiliar, although intelligible, sentences. She must allow that it was possible for me to come to believe, even to know, that Caesar divided Gaul into three parts, on coming upon this proposition for the very first time.

New sentences, or the utterances of hitherto unheard sentences, cannot be elements in a regularly experienced conjunction that has given rise to an association in the subject's mind. So if an empirical association really plays the key part that Hume thinks it does in testimonial inference, we must locate it elsewhere. It seems that the association will have to be between testimony, considered generally, and actuality, considered generally. This, surely, is what Hume himself was gesturing towards when he remarked:

> The reason, why we place any credit in witnesses and historians, is not derived from any connexion, which we perceive *a priori*, between testimony and reality, but because we are accustomed to find a conformity between them . . .
> (Hume 1975: X.i, 112)

On this view, the significant feature of the first term of the correlation will be the utterance-*type*, irrespective of its content: the fact that it is testimony. The idea is that utterances of this (testimonial) type, no matter what their content, correlate well with reality. So the empirical correlation that Hume's associationist theory demands holds at a very high level of generality, between utterance-type and actuality. We learn, from experience, that testimonies correlate well with how things actually are. This is how we get into the business of learning from testimony in the first place.

And now, to complete our account of testimonial inference as conceived by Hume, we need to add that the content of the utterance, whatever it may be, specifies the actuality that the hearer comes to believe in. You say, in testimonial mode as I understand it, "There's honey for tea" and thereupon I begin to believe – even to know – that there's honey for tea. Association alone, which according to Hume is the engine of inductive inferences, cannot get me to the belief *that there's honey for tea* from your say-so. In the context of specifically testimonial inference, its role can only be to get me to the point of believing in some actuality or other on the basis of your say-so. So we need to add to the account that, in the context of testimony, content is preserved: what I get to believe is precisely what you told me. With other speech-acts, even other indicative speech-acts, content is not preserved. There is no pressure on me to accept that the facts are as specified by the sense of your utterance, if I take you to be hazarding a guess. With testimony, however, I *am* under a constraint to believe what you say. It is not a binding constraint, of course; it is more like what Hume elsewhere calls a "gentle force" (Hume 1978: I, i, iv, 10): more of this later, too.

This completes my interpretation of how Hume fits testimonial inferences into the general framework of his empiricism. The central thought is that just as I have become accustomed to associate smoke with fire, so I have become accustomed to associate testimony as such with reality as such, and thus, through experience, I have acquired a general propensity to believe what I am told. Hume, in fact, thinks that, under certain circumstances, this propensity is often moderated. In "Weighing testimony" (pp. 88ff.), we shall see how and when this happens; as we just now remarked, the constraint to believe what we are told is not totally binding. For the present, let me say just this: not only is this, as I think, how, in broad terms, Hume sees things; I also think it is pretty much how things actually are: the truth of the matter. This view has been severely attacked, however. I shall now argue that the attack misfires.

In defence of the Humean approach

The attack that I have in mind is largely due to C. A. J. Coady. His summary statement of Hume's position fits our interpretation well. He puts it as follows:

> We rely upon testimony as a species of evidence *because* each of us observes for himself a constant and regular conjunction between what people report and the way the world is.
>
> (1992: 82)

Coady claims that this position is not sustainable and that Hume was completely wrong to suggest, as we have just seen him suggesting, that there is no "connexion, which we perceive *a priori*, between testimony and reality". According to Coady, if, as Hume claims, I *learn* through experience that testimony is reliable by observing a conformity between people's testimonies and actualities and thus coming to associate them, I must "understand what testimony is independently of knowing that it is, in any degree, a reliable form of evidence" (1992: 85). In other words, I must be able to identify testimonies *as such* if I am to discover that they match up well with the facts (supposing they do). A child might be able to identify smoke *as such* while not appreciating its relation to fire and vice versa; so for her it can be an empirical discovery that smoke correlates well with fire. Similarly, so it is said, if there is no reason a priori for me to expect that testimony and actuality generally match, my initial position will be one in which, as I think, my observations may reveal no significant correlation between what I independently identify as testimonies and fact. Coady, however, claims that we cannot conceive that this outcome might be possible: in the absence of correlation, I could have no proper concept of *testimony* at all, no reason to suspect that any noises I heard *were* testimony – the kind of utterances whose use is to inform other people of the facts; without some significant degree of correlation there could be no foundation for the very idea of testimony. On the Humean hypothesis, so it seems, we could imagine an alien world in which testimony was as common as in our world but rarely matched the facts, a world in which people regularly misinformed one another. But this idea is incoherent. In the absence of correlation we could have no reason to think that any of the noises people uttered in this imagined world were testimony. Misinforming, misreporting, cannot be the norm. Testimony, therefore, considered as a species of evidence, cannot be assimilated, Humewise, to ordinary empirical evidence. It cannot be an empirical fact that testimonies tend to correspond with reality. Rather it is an a priori truth, and testimony, therefore, is a distinct sort of evidence; it is *sui generis*. Hume's so-called "reductionism", which views testimony as if it were a form of inductive evidence, is a great mistake.

This argument has been widely endorsed by Hume's enemies, and Coady is, surely, right in holding that the practice of testimony can only exist on condition that the facts should be, more often than not, as they are (testimonially) said to be. We cannot conceive that we might discover it to be otherwise since any such "discovery" would serve to undermine the idea that it was *testimony* we were investigating. But Hume is not vulnerable to this argument. Coady's summary of the Humean position envisages a certain kind of history underpinning the association we come to make between testimony and reality, a history to which Hume is not committed. It pictures an innocent beginner first identifying samples of testimony *as such* and then discovering that there's a good correlation between testimonies thus identified and the facts they are taken to report. This scenario does entail the possibility that no significant correlation between testimony and reality might be found. But there is no reason to think it is Hume's.

Hume, I suggest, pictures our innocent more realistically, as being born into a world (our world) where what we cognoscenti call "testimony" is abundant and does match up pretty well, on the whole, with fact. For example, when the child's parents say "Dog!" more often than not there's a dog, and so on. Certainly, a child born into a world where this was not true could never form the idea of testimony and, I daresay, never master language. But a Humean theory of testimony does not require that a child should *first* identify utterances as being of the informative kind (testimony) and *then* discover there's a fit between testimony and reality. The idea might be that it notices, often in somewhat staged situations, a correlation between as yet uncategorized utterances and facts – dog when the noise "dog" is emitted – and from that develops both its idea of testimony and its understanding of the sense of the word *dog*. There *are* reasons a priori for thinking that there will be a significant correlation between testimonies and the facts which testimonies report; the scenario which requires that we can conceive that we might discover there is none *is* absurd. But why should we think it is Hume's scenario? Its absurdity has no tendency to show that we did not each of us individually come by the very idea of testimony through experience, by observing that what we eventually come to recognize as testimonies correlate pretty well with how things are. Of course, it is not just a happy chance that we are able to develop an idea of testimony in this way. No doubt, evolution has wired the capacity to learn about testimony into our brains. It brings us great benefits. But Hume can accept this. He does not think our minds are featureless at birth, blank slates; he believes in human nature.

Compare what we might call *natural evidence*. By this I mean just the sorts of things that trigger inductive inferences as conceived by Hume. So smoke is (natural) evidence of fire. Now no one supposes that Hume was committed to the idea that in infancy we confront the world with a ready made notion of *evidence* and then discover empirically that there is a fit between evidence *in general* and reality. On the contrary, surely we each of us develop the idea of evidence in experiencing regular conjunctions of one type of thing with another. Certainly, we could not have acquired this notion of *evidence* if there weren't a correlation between individual bits of evidence and the things they are supposedly evidence for. The world has to be regular if we are to acquire our inferential habits. But this has no tendency to show that we do not acquire our notion of evidence, through experience, in tandem with our acquisition of a multitude of inductive beliefs. So, too, with "testimonial evidence".

We should not pursue the analogy too far, however. Hume's theory of inductive inference gives no role to the *idea* of evidence. If I am not mistaken, the situation is different with testimony. Recognition of a speech-act as being of the testimonial or informative kind is essential to the experienced hearer's testimonial inference. But this is not inconsistent with the thought that we originally acquire the idea of testimony in experience.

Weighing testimony

If this account of how Hume thinks testimony and the beliefs it engenders fit into the general framework of his empiricism is correct, we must ask why he has been widely misunderstood. Part of the answer lies in the use of the word *inference* we noted earlier. That encourages modern readers to think in terms of explicit reasoning from evidence to a conclusion, and they may think that, on the Humean view, such reasoning occurs even in the most elementary case of getting to believe (know) something from testimony. This way of looking at the matter is then apt to be reinforced by Hume's most sustained discussion of testimony and the one that naturally has most captured the attention of his readers.

This is his discussion of miracles in the first *Enquiry*. Now, it is important that in this section he writes as a philosophical historian interested in the principles by which testimony should be evaluated from a historian's point of view. It is a mistake to think he is commenting on what he conceives to be the basic way of receiving testimony. For a historian, supposedly miraculous events are especially problematic. A wise man, Hume tells us,

> proportions his belief to the evidence. In such conclusions as are founded on an infallible experience [he means an *exceptionless* series of experiences of one type of event always being followed by another], he expects the event with the last degree of assurance, and regards his past experience as a full proof of the future existence of that event. In other cases, he proceeds with more caution: He weighs the opposite experiments: He considers which side is supported by the greater number of experiments: To that side he inclines, with doubt and hesitation; and when at last he fixes his judgment, the evidence exceeds not what we properly call probability. All probability, then, supposes an opposition of experiments and observations, where the one side is found to overbalance the other, and to produce a degree of evidence, proportioned to the superiority.
> (1975: X.i, 110)

The problem with reports of untoward events, like miracles, is that there is always going to be an "opposition of experiments and observations". That is what makes the events untoward. And, human nature being what it is, an audience that is aware of this "opposition" will not accept the testimony unhesitatingly, in the way that we do accept the testimony of tide tables, say, or lunar calendars. The effect of contrary experiments is to cause an audience to suspend its natural response to testimony, to weigh it rather than simply to accept it. You do not accept what you are told, just like that, if you have independent reason to think that what you are told may be false or at least is unlikely to be true. In other words, you don't accept it uncritically if it is manifestly out of line with what you already believe. In such a case, something must give: either you abandon your antecedent belief(s) or you decline to believe what the testimony reports, or perhaps you find some more sophisticated way of reconciling the conflict by modifying the conflicting propositions. Once a piece of testimony falls under question it has to be evaluated and balanced against other evidence.

Miracles are especially problematic. Hume thinks that the only currently available evidence for the occurrence of any miracle is going to be in the form of testimony: the report of an eyewitness, or perhaps the report of a report of an eyewitness. His contention is that it will always be more probable that the testimony is false, on account of the testifier's error, deceit, gullible love of the marvellous and so on, than that something actually happened that contravenes all experience. His position is not that miracles don't or can't happen; rather, it can never be sensible to believe that one did happen. Faced with a report of a miracle we should suspect the reporter's sincerity or her competence.

Now what concerns us here is the way in which the notion of testimony is deployed in the argument. The vital point is this: the idea of evaluating a bit of testimony, of weighing up whether or not to accept it, presupposes that acceptance is, as it were, the *default* response to testimony. The question, often prompted by reports of events that seem extraordinary, is whether to deliver the default response or override it. It may be prompted in other ways, too. As Hume writes:

> This contrariety of evidence . . . may be derived from several different causes; from the opposition of contrary testimony; from the character or number of the witnesses; from the

manner of their delivering their testimony; or from the union of all these circumstances. We entertain a suspicion concerning any matter of fact, when the witnesses contradict each other; when they are but few, or of a doubtful character; when they have an interest in what they affirm; when they deliver their testimony with hesitation, or on the contrary, with too violent asseverations. There are many other particulars of the same kind, which may diminish or destroy the force of any argument, derived from human testimony.   (1975: X.i, 112–13)

Critics of Hume such as Coady, it seems to me, have tended to mistake a discussion of the questions of when and how testimony should be weighed or evaluated, when the default response should be withheld, for a theory of how testimony should be received in the first place. They can then contrast Hume rather neatly with his contemporary and critic, Thomas Reid, whose understanding of testimony was, allegedly, quite different.

According to Reid, we are divinely endowed with what he calls the Principle of Credulity, which disposes us to accept what we are told without question. In other words, the natural (default) response to testimony is to accept it; that is how God has made us. Happily, God has matched this principle with another, the Principle of Veracity, which ensures that testimonies are generally true. So we can be sure that the beliefs we get from testimony, in virtue of the Principle of Credulity, will, for the most part, be true (Reid 1970: Ch. 6 §24). Summing this up, one recent commentator says that Reid "treats testimony as 'innocent' (i.e., trustworthy) unless shown guilty"; Hume, by contrast, allegedly "treats it as 'guilty' (i.e., not worthy of belief) until a good track-record is shown" (Stevenson 1993: 436). I think this is quite wrong. Both Hume and Reid recognize a natural propensity in human beings to believe what they are told; according to Reid this propensity is due to divine providence and according to Hume it is acquired through our registering a correspondence between the content of some speech-acts and reality (Hume 1975: X.i, 112). According to Reid, it is fortunately matched, again thanks to divine providence, by an independent "tallying" Principle of Veracity; according to Hume, we acquire the habit of believing *because* we have become aware that some speech-acts correlate well with reality. We come to view those speech-acts as testimonial. Hume and Reid are pretty much agreed on the manifest facts of human nature; their difference is over the question how we come to have the natural propensities we do. But there is, in general, rather a high degree of convergence between them. Just as Hume thinks that the propensity to believe testimonies, born of experience, may be moderated in the light of experience, so Reid thinks that the Principle of Credulity "is unlimited in children, until they meet with instances of deceit and falsehood: and it retains a very considerable degree of strength through life" (Reid 1970: 240). For both, experience breeds suspicion and causes us to view some testimonies askance. For both, the natural or default response to a bit of testimony is to accept it.

Ways of learning from testimony

Let us summarize what we can learn from this debate. If I am not mistaken, Hume, no less than Reid, thinks there is a natural way of responding to what is perceived as testimony. Hume thinks that experience conditions us to deliver this response, whereas Reid thinks this mode of behaviour is divinely implanted; but however it is to be explained, both think it is part of our human nature to behave in this way. The response in question is simply to *accept* the information contained in the testimonies to which we are exposed. It seems pretty clear that this is how it is with us in many situations: for example, when we read the price tags on goods in the shops, lists of ingredients on pharmaceuticals, signposts, and so on. This is the default response to testimony; we accept that P on being told that P simply in virtue of understanding that we *are* being told that P. Nevertheless, we are sometimes suspicious. We *may* want to draw the line at believing reports of miracles, just like that. Where each of us draws the line will be at least to some extent a function of our previous experience, although some of us may be temperamentally more inclined to be suspicious than others. Hume's celebrated discussion of miracles is largely a discussion about how and where we draw this line.

If we withhold the default response to a bit of testimony we may begin to treat it differently. Not necessarily, since we may just reject the testimony. But there are many steps short of outright rejection.

We may begin to weigh up how likely the speaker is to have known the truth, how likely she is to be deceiving us and so on. We begin to apply, as it were, a calculus of probabilities to the testimony. At the end of such a process, we may conclude that it is more likely than not, or quite likely, or just possible that P: what we were told in the first place. But this outcome is not obtained simply in virtue of *understanding* the speech-act we were confronted with. The speech-act itself has become a subject of explicit reasoning. Those who accuse Hume of reductivism, the failure to appreciate the *sui genericity* of testimony considered as evidence, are saying, in effect, that for Hume the default response to a bit of testimony is to apply a calculus of probabilities to it. I think they are wrong.

Remarkably, what neither Hume, nor Reid, nor any other philosopher to my knowledge has tried to spell out is how exactly testimony works, what exactly we *understand* when we deliver the default response to a bit of testimony just in virtue of understanding it *as* testimony. That is the matter to which I now turn. It will reveal as much about the nature of knowledge as about testimony.

The concept of knowledge: 6 a new theory

Preamble

If I am right, neither Hume nor Reid thinks that the default response to a bit of testimony is to weigh it in the way that one might weigh a bit of inductive evidence. That response is sometimes elicited by special circumstances; there may be reasons for doubting the speaker's sincerity, in any case there may be reasons for thinking that the events she reports may not be true, there may be conflicts of testimony, and so on. In such circumstances it will be appropriate for a hearer to engage her critical faculties in order to assess the evidential value of the testimony she has been faced with. But this is not the basic kind of response, the default. Neither Hume nor Reid attempts to work out the basic testimonial process; they simply take it for granted that we often come by information through testimony, but they do not ask how. This is the subject to which I now turn.

A good place to begin is to ask what, at bottom, testimony is for. My suggestion is this. Human beings, like other more or less intelligent locomotors, need true beliefs for the successful conduct of their lives. We need them, above all, in order to realize our desires and bring our projects to successful conclusions. All our actions have to be performed in the circumstances that we believe to obtain, and it matters that our beliefs be true, if the actions are to be successful. But human beings are exceptional: the variety of goals we can conceive for ourselves and our capacity for an indefinitely wide range of cooperative endeavours that require us to share information with other people are vastly greater than other creatures seem able to encompass. We have correspondingly greater informational needs. So it is no accident that we have evolved special means for satisfying those needs, that is, for getting the multitude of true beliefs necessary for our flourishing. In particular we have developed ways of exploiting the work of one another by means of linguistic communication, so that each of us can benefit from observations and discoveries made by other people and we can share information to our mutual advantage. This is the origin of testimony. To be sure, we are not the only creatures that communicate, but no others can match us in the range and detail of the information we are capable of conveying to one another and in the fine focus with which we can articulate our informational wants.

The question is, how do we do it? How exactly does testimony work to provide us with beliefs we may need? It seems, on the whole, that philosophers have not even noticed that there *is* a question here. In Chapter 5 I suggested that it is an essential element in the process that the person who hears (or reads) a testimonial utterance should understand it *as* testimony. But what does this understanding involve? And when a speaker recognizes a speech-act as testimony, what does this recognition imply for her response? In what follows I am going to sketch out the broad lineaments of the theory that I think is lacking.

We are going to be concerned with what we may call "testimonial transitions":

(TT) $$U_S P \rightarrow B_H P$$

Here a speaker, S, produces an utterance with the content P, and a hearer, H, thereupon forms a belief with content P. How come? I think that there is a whole spectrum of possible hearer responses to what is correctly perceived as a testimonial utterance, which may mediate this transition: they range from something close to a primitive animal uptake of information to something very much more sophisticated. There are also off-beat cases where a hearer ends up with a belief that P through misapprehending the nature of the speech-act, as when a reader, in Hume's example, mistakes a novel for a history or for some other reason.

My idea about knowledge is that the concept of knowledge emerged, when human beings learnt to reflect on this process by which they benefit from the observations of their fellows, as the concept of what provides its underlying rationale; and because this is so, it is unsurprising that the concept should sometimes feature explicitly, somewhere towards the more sophisticated end of the spectrum of possible hearer responses, as an element in the mechanism of transmission.

Speech-acts

It will be helpful, first, to say more about the notion of a speech-act, to which we have already helped ourselves. It was introduced into philosophy by J. L. Austin, or at least he coined the phrase and was the first to theorize about the topic in a systematic way (Austin 1962). It would take us off course to examine all the theoretical complications of his insight, but the basic idea is important for us. Historically, philosophers have been inclined to assume that making statements of fact which may be assessed as either true or false is the primary or central use of language and they have largely overlooked the omnipresent phenomenon of speech-acts. Of course, they can hardly have failed to notice that we do other things with language besides state facts. For example, *obviously* we also ask questions and issue commands; do we not produce utterances in the interrogative and imperative moods as well as in the indicative? But philosophers on the whole have hardly registered the rich variety of speech-act types we are capable of, or even the range of types that utterances in any one of these different grammatical moods may instantiate. To take one key example of the kind of speech-act that first excited Austin's interest, an utterance of the indicative sentence "I name this ship *Titanic*", in the right circumstances by a duly appointed person, would not be used with the primary purpose of conveying the (no doubt true) information that she is naming the ship *Titanic*; the utterance of this sentence (in the right circumstances and so on) constitutes the very act of naming itself. And if someone wishes to insist that nevertheless the speaker who utters it also says something that can be evaluated as true or false, we shall have to say that what makes it true, if that is the correct evaluation, is that the speaker, being duly appointed, in uttering the sentence in the appropriate circumstances, is thereby naming the ship *Titanic*. Part of the task of a philosopher who wants to develop a proper theory of speech-acts will be to investigate the various kinds of conditions under which this action will have been successfully executed, and the different ways in which an utterance of the naming sentence may fail to name the ship properly or fail to name anything at all. And similarly for hosts of other speech-acts.

Now, we are going to be concerned specifically with the speech-act of informing, or telling another person some fact. And we need to remember that if I utter the indicative sentence "The cat is on the mat" in order to tell you that the cat is on the mat, there is nothing in what I say that reveals that I am telling you this fact, in the way that "I name . . ." indicates that I am naming. Sometimes, for special purposes, we say things like "I am telling you that the cat is on the mat", but this is not the norm; normally, hearers have to interpret the nature of the speech-acts they are exposed to for themselves, guided by context and other cues. The normal way of telling some-one that the cat is on the mat is in fact to say just that: to utter "The cat is on the mat", or some equivalent sentence. But this utterance, considered apart from any context, in and by itself, could just as well be an overt guess, the expression of a hunch, a philosophical exam-ple or even a question, and so on. Since there is nothing in the utter-ance as such to tell us what sort of speech-act it is, it has been rather easy for philosophers, whose attention has often been fixed on big issues about truth and reality, to overlook the whole business of speech-acts or at least to lump different kinds of speech-act into extremely broad categories, such as those suggested by grammar: imperatives, indicatives, interrogatives, optatives, and so on. In fact, until quite recently, philosophers have hardly been concerned at all with the dynamic aspects of normal human conversational exchanges. No doubt the Cartesian ideal of the solitary enquirer inventing a secure science by her own unaided efforts has a lot to answer for here. If a philosopher's dominant interest is to work out how such a Robinson Crusoe representation of reality is to be obtained and secured against doubt, they will hardly be interested in how different individuals communicate with one another, and how they respond to one another's communications.

Speech-acts, for the most part at least, are what Thomas Reid called "social acts" and contrasted with "solitary acts". By *social acts* he understands such operations as necessarily suppose an intercourse with some other intelligent being. A man may understand and will ... though he should know of no intelligent being in the universe beside himself. But, when he asks for information, or receives it; when he bears testimony, or receives the testimony of another; when he asks a favour or accepts one ... – these are acts of social intercourse between intelligent beings, and can have no place in solitude. ... They are neither simple apprehension, nor judgment, nor reasoning, nor are they any combination of these operations.

(Reid 1863: Essay I, Ch. 8)

In Reid's view, the misrepresentation of social acts as solitary acts is a prime source of philosophical error: the misrepresentation of a speaker's act of informing, say, as the expression of a judgement, or a hearer's acceptance of information as something that involves a kind of solitary reasoning upon evidence. It is in the nature of speech-acts to be social: that is, they typically assume an audience and they look for responses from their audience that are appropriate for the kind of act in question, much as the performance of certain steps in a dance triggers a partner to perform appropriate steps in response. Their social nature becomes manifest through their systematic connection with specific types of hearer's response. This is not to say that what are essentially social acts cannot ever be performed in solitude, and perhaps performed without an audience even being intended: Samuel Pepys's diaries contain many acts of informative telling that were, in the peculiar circumstances of their composition, never intended to inform an audience, unless perhaps they were intended to inform Pepys himself at a later stage of life. But Pepys could never have performed these speech-acts had there not been a public practice of informing other people of the facts which he was able to appropriate for his private ends.

For Reid, the following philosophical account of how a testimonial transition (TT) is effected perfectly exhibits the kind of error he is keen to expose – the explication of a social act of telling or informing as if it were a solitary act:

(1) From S's saying P we infer S believes that P is true. (2) From the fact that S believes P is true, we infer that S has been

exposed to evidence for P. (3) From the fact that there is evidence for P, we infer P.

(Harman 1990: 47, variables altered
to conform to my conventions)

Here we seem to see a solitary thinker who is confronted with an indicative utterance, treating it as a bit of empirical evidence from which she draws out a string of inferences to the conclusion that P (= the content of the utterance). One is inclined to ask whatever happened to *telling*? But there are many solitarist scenarios like this in the philosophical literature. For example, there is that devised by Goldman for fitting testimony into the chain of reasons and causes, which, on his view, would warrant counting the belief that the hearer ends up with as knowledge (p. 60), or the crude "Humean" model (not, I think, Hume's) described by Mellor (p. 81). Of course, these theorists do not necessarily suppose that anyone *explicitly* reasons in the way they suggest; but perhaps they do think they have reconstructed the rationale that underlies a hearer's favourable response to testimony.

In all these cases we have to picture the hearer, on being told that P, consciously or unconsciously reasoning her way, all on her own, to the conclusion that P; we see her treating S's utterance not as a social act expecting a specific kind of response from the hearer, but as a solitary act that constitutes a bit evidence for the hearer; the hearer then must reason her own way to a conclusion using essentially the same sort of method as a solitary scientist might use as she works her way to a plausible hypothesis on the basis of what she has observed through her microscope. In Chapter 5 I argued that it isn't like this. Our task now is to work out how it really is.

I shall begin with some remarks about a different kind of speech-act altogether: not telling someone what is the case, but telling some-one to do something – ordering, commanding. This is a speech-act whose social character we pretty well understand. My aim is to use our familiarity with it to awaken our instinctive understanding of what social acts involve and, in particular, the type of informative acts that primarily concerns us. (It is, incidentally, no accident, as I think, that the same word, *tell*, is used in both these senses, telling someone to do something and telling someone the facts; they both connect with the idea of authority. However, I do not build on this apparent connection. I comment on imperative telling simply to illustrate, with what is already familiar, what the social nature of speech-acts involves.)

So, we are going to be concerned with a certain class of utterances in the imperative mood. Characteristically an utterance in this mood specifies an action and, to put it with necessary vagueness, looks for the performance of the specified action by the intended audience. Imperative utterances are not exclusively used for issuing orders or commands, but when they are used for this purpose the response they look for is *obedience*. There are other possibilities and the responses then looked for are different, according to the speech-act for which they are used. For example, if, in uttering the imperative sentence "Pass the salt", I am making a request, it isn't exactly *obedience* I want from my neighbour, although I surely hope that she will comply with my request. Again, if I say, "Go for it!", by way of giving advice, I may be more or less indifferent whether my audience actually acts on my advice and perhaps the most I look for is that they consider it. It would be idle to try to produce a definitive taxonomy of the speech-acts which we can perform by uttering imperative sentences; in real life our intentions and our understandings are often very subtly nuanced. Perhaps all these speech-acts, in some way or other, look for, or somehow solicit, action on the part of the audience; but the way that ordering, requesting, urging, recommending, entreating, advising and so on look for action is very varied.

Suppose you say to me "Pass the salt", and I pass the salt; is this a case of obedience, compliance or what? Just as there may be nothing in the utterance as such that reveals whether the speech-act is to be understood as a command, a request, or whatever, so there may be nothing in the response as such that reveals whether the hearer is obeying, complying or what. If we have met, as social equals, at table, I shall most likely interpret your utterance as a request and my response as compliance; and that perhaps matches your intention. But relationships are not always equal. Maybe you are my stern Victorian parent and I am your poor repressed child: then perhaps we shall both understand you to be ordering and me to be obeying. Or perhaps you are the head of my department and I am your obsequious assistant; then the situation may be unclear – you conceive yourself to be requesting on the grounds that we are all equal at table, and I conceive myself to be obeying because I am incorrigibly deferential. What is clear is that commands look for obedience and requests look for something different, like compliance. But it is often possible for a hearer to misread the speaker's intention, and in some situations the speaker's intention may not be perfectly clear even to herself; if I fail to pass the salt to my superior she may begin to see herself more as having ordered, or at least as having the right to be *obeyed*, whereas if I had passed it she might have been content to think she had made a request.

Commanding and obedience are bound together by the idea of a hierarchy in which the superior person can enjoin actions on the inferior. It may be a hierarchy of physical power. The armed thief says "Lie on the floor" and I obey because his weapon gives him power over me. Or, more usually perhaps, it may be an institutional hierarchy in which the superior person has authority to enjoin actions upon their inferior. But, of course, institutional hierarchies are quite often backed by power, so the boundaries between force and moral or political authority are not always clear. When I obey you I thereby acknowledge that you, in virtue of your superiority, however it may be grounded, are empowered to tell me to do whatever it may be, in the expectation that I will do it. As we have seen, however, it does not follow from the fact that I performed the action you ordered that I was obeying you. It would not, properly speaking, be *obedience* if I thought I was complying out of goodwill with what was no more than a request. In these circumstances, of course, you might mistakenly think that I was obeying you, so that the misunderstanding might never come to light. Again, if I fail to do what you ordered, there are various possibilities. Maybe I realize that you were ordering me, but I reject your implied claim to have the authority or power to do so. Alternatively, I realize that you issued an order and I recognize your authority to do so, but I deliberately flout it; or else I conceive of myself as declining to comply with what I took to be a request. And, of course, you and I may disagree over which description fits my doing or failing to do the action in question, depending on how we individually conceive of the speech-act and your right to execute it.

Finally, when a speaker orders someone to perform a certain action she intends that the hearer perform that action. The performance is necessary if the speaker's intention is to be consummated. But this is something that is outside the speaker's power. Consummation requires the hearer's collaboration and that may be withheld. This is another aspect of the sociality of this speech-act, that its consummation involves both speaker and hearer. This point, about the place of the hearer's will in the business, will turn out to be very significant when the business is informative telling. To that I now turn.

Telling the facts

The aim of this digression about imperative telling was to bring home, with reference to what is familiar, the point that particular kinds of speech-act look for particular kinds of response from the audience to which they are addressed and will not be properly consummated if they fail to receive the looked for response. Furthermore, it may not always be manifest from the words that are uttered exactly which kind of speech-act is being performed and hence which kind of response is sought. As we have just seen, even within the domain of imperative utterances there is plenty of scope for ambiguity and misunderstanding and thus for mismatch between speaker's intention and hearer's response.

Now to return to our original question: how is the testimonial transition

$$(TT) \qquad\qquad U_S P \rightarrow B_H P$$

effected? Let us begin with some relatively uncontroversial points. Most theorists, of whatever persuasion, are likely to subscribe to something like the following list of conditions for a speaker's testimony that P engendering the knowledge, or at least a high quality belief, that P in a hearer. These are necessary conditions; there is no claim that they are, either singly or jointly, sufficient, not least because they make no mention of what will turn out to be crucially significant – how the hearer responds to the testimony.

1. P must be true. This perhaps is the one entirely undisputed condition.
2. The speaker who produces the testimonial speech-act must be sincere. This means, in the first place, that she must believe that what she tells her audience is true. But this is not a sufficient

condition of sincerity. Consider the case of double bluff. The double bluffer believes that what she says is true but tries, through the manner of her telling, to secure that her audience won't believe it. This speaker can hardly be described as sincere and I doubt anyone would think that either knowledge or even a good quality belief could be obtained *from* a source which is so contaminated by deceit; but this is not to say that a hearer who reasonably suspected double bluff might not reason her way from the suspected bluff to the truth of what was said and obtain a good quality belief that way. Sincerity, as well as requiring that the speaker believe that what she says is true, also requires that she is not making an improper use of the speech-act that she performs. Any decision about what, precisely, that might involve will turn on how speech-acts, of whichever sort are in question, are understood. Finally, we should also note, in this connection, that there are plenty of non-testimonial speech-acts, performed by utterances in the indicative mood, whose sincere performance, as with telling, requires that the speaker believe that what she says is true. For example, if I am asked my opinion about the outcome of the next election, I should be insincere if what I said did not correspond with my belief; but I am in no position to *tell* you what the outcome will be. If I were to tell you this, the sincerity condition requires that, in addition to believing that what I tell you is true, I also believe I am *competent* to tell you (whatever this may involve).

3. Not only must the speaker think she is competent, but she must *be* competent to tell her audience that P. Some people may tell you things with perfect sincerity when in fact they are not competent to do so. This is the case with Meno, in the dialogue that bears his name. He is prepared, with evident sincerity, to tell people about virtue but, according to Plato, lacks the necessary competence (see p. 10). Precisely what being competent involves will depend on whatever theory is favoured. Perhaps those who are incompetent do not have adequate justifying reasons for believing that P. Or perhaps they are not in a position to know in the sense that they do not stand in the right kind of causal relation to the fact of the matter. Or perhaps they are defective in some other way.

One recent and influential author, Elizabeth Fricker, has made much of these two requirements of sincerity and competence. On her view, the fact that these are part of what our common-sense understanding of what the process demands, if a hearer is to get to know that P from hearing a speaker's assertion that P, provides support for a justificationist analysis of knowledge (Fricker 1987). I believe my own explanation of the nature of knowledge accommodates these common-sense requirements better. Fricker's notion of competence, in fact, is virtually tantamount to knowledge: on her account, you are competent with respect to P only if your believing that P entails that P is true; or, in other words, if you are competent as regards P, you can't be wrong about it (Fricker 1987). It is very plausible to say that you can only obtain the knowledge that P from someone's say-so if they know that P. But, as will appear, I maintain that this indicates a quite different kind of mechanism for the acquisition of knowledge from say-so than that favoured by a justificationist.

However, I go along with Fricker in holding that the transition in (TT) is mediated through the hearer's understanding of the speech-act. Here is her account:

> a *speaker*, believing that P, and wishing to communicate this belief, makes an utterance which constitutes his asserting that P; his audience, a *hearer*, observing and understanding it – that is to say, recognising it as the speech-act that it is – as a result comes also to believe that P.   (Fricker 1987: 68–9)

I agree. But more needs to be said by way of clarification and amplification.

Suppose that S, being strongly of the opinion that P, utters the indicative sentence "P". The hearer, H, recognizes that S's intention just *is* to voice a strongly held opinion; she is not *telling* anyone that P but she wants to make her own conviction evident. Recognizing that this is the nature of S's speech-act ("recognising it as the speech-act that it is"), H consequently comes to believe that P. This is a feasible scenario, and it satisfies Fricker's (thin) description of what happens in a successful case of what she calls "assertion". But it is not a case where H begins to believe that P on understanding that she has been *told* that P; on the contrary, she recognizes that S was only giving voice to her strong conviction. What we have here is an instance of what we might call the guru effect; H is disposed to accept *this* speaker's opinion about virtually anything and consequently adopts this opinion for herself. Maybe she is in awe of S and views her opinions about no matter what with obsequious admiration. Perhaps Fricker might want to deny that voicing opinions, even forcibly voicing strongly held opinions, counts as *assertion* in the relevant sense. But this only serves to emphasize that, if the transition in (TT) is mediated through the hearer's understanding S's speech-act, we are owed an account of what assertion in the relevant sense is and what understanding it, therefore, might entail.

Could her idea be that in *proper* cases of testimony the hearer comes by her belief simply in virtue of understanding the speech-act as testimony, unaided by special ancillary dispositions, such as the disposition to adopt uncritically the opinions of *this* speaker? The hearer recognizes that the speaker's intention is to inform, to tell her that P or (as we often say) to let her know that P, and in virtue of understanding this she begins to believe that P herself; in the other case, however, a hearer could perfectly well understand the speech-act for what it is (an expression of opinion) and not end up believing that P since she might think this speaker's opinions had no special claim on her attention. If this is Fricker's view it would not be unlike Hume's position as I interpret it, or Thomas Reid's. The thought is that there is a general disposition that we all share to accept the testimony of other people. Given this predisposition, perhaps *all* that is required for the hearer to obtain the belief that P from a speaker's telling her that P is that she should understand the speech-act *as* testimony that P.

This account is on the right track, but, as it stands, it is too simple. As both Hume and Reid saw, we regularly exercise judgement about both the credibility of informants and the credibility of their information, when prompted by special features of particular cases. We make assessments of their sincerity and their competence and thus come to believe some of the things we are told and to reject other things or else withhold judgement on the question of whether to accept or reject. This is because we are aware of the possibility of deceit or error on the part of speakers. As suggested in Chapter 5, the situation seems to be more like this: the *default* response to testimony is to accept what we are told, but, as is the way with defaults, this response may be overridden. What Hume called "contrary experiments" alert us to the possibility that the speaker, for one reason or another, may have got it wrong and that may prompt us to override the default.

As far as this account goes, I believe it is correct, but it may be objected that it leaves a crucial question unanswered: what exactly is it that *distinguishes* telling someone that P from (merely) expressing a strongly held conviction that P, with the consequence that acceptance of what is said is the appropriate uptake in the one case but not in the other? That question has a very short answer: it is a brute fact that the speech-act of informing or telling looks for this response. There is no further for the account to go. An equally short answer would be appropriate if someone asked what it is that distinguishes ordering someone to do something from, say, entreating them to do it, so that obedience is appropriate in the one case but not the other. To order *is* to look for obedience. You don't first learn what ordering is and then learn what the looked for response is. There is only one lesson to learn; that is the nature of social acts. Similarly, to tell someone that P *is* to look for acceptance that P on their part. This is the real reason why, as Austin once put it, "If I have said I know, you insult me in a special way by refusing to accept it" (Austin 1961: 68). In refusing to accept what I say you impugn me (my sincerity or my competence); and in fact I don't have to say "I know", I just have to *tell* you something.

By default, then, a hearer's understanding a speech-act as one of informative telling is evinced by her simply accepting what the speaker says, admitting it into the body of her beliefs; and to deliver this response to what is intended as a declaration of firm belief rather than as an act of informing or telling is either to misunderstand the speech-act or perhaps to evince something like guru-fixation. In the latter case we should speak rather of agreeing that P than of accepting that P.

Now, the point about a default response is that it can be overridden when circumstances require it. Contrast the case of bees. It is widely known that foraging honey bees, on returning to their hive, often perform a kind of dance, aspects of which correlate very closely with the distance and orientation of the food source they have been visiting. Other bees in the hive, observing the dance, fly to that source of food and forage there for themselves. The dance, it seems, encodes information that the attendant bees understand and act on. Here, however, the idea of a default response can't get a grip. There are no circumstances in which an attendant bee might override its natural response to the dance. It cannot think anything like: I don't believe these foragers; there's no nectar in that direction; it's either a con or they are confused. It cannot think, period; and it cannot operate with the notion of possible error, which is the conceptual pre-condition of being able to contemplate overriding the default. Despite what some linguisticists have written, bee behaviour is just that: behaviour, not language. The fact that information is encoded in the dance doesn't mean that the bees are telling one another (indicatively) that there is food over there, or telling one another (imperatively) to fly in such and such a direction, or however else someone might be disposed to interpret the dance. This is not to say that the human institution of telling may not be an evolutionary descendant of something much more primitive, the sort of adaptation that bees exhibit, in virtue of which people can be informed beneficially about food or threats or whatever by other people. Something of the sort must, surely, be true. What distinguishes evolved human beings, however, is that we are conscious creatures, capable of reflecting on what we are doing and thinking critically about our engagement in the business of communicating information. Specifically we are aware of the possibility of misinformation. So, as Reid and Hume both appreciated, we are capable of overriding the natural responses to informative acts; they are, for us, not a behavioural necessity, as they are for the bees, but a default, which we may choose to override.

This is not to say that human responses to acts of telling (both imperative and indicative) may not be immediate and more or less automatic. On being told to stand to attention, the trained soldier on parade obeys instantly. He doesn't think: the sergeant wants me to stand to attention; the sergeant has the power to penalize me if I don't, so perhaps it would be prudent to stand to attention. And the child who has latched on to the game of informative telling, on being told "That's a dog", doesn't usually pause to ask herself whether her informant is credible or the information plausible. In particular, she doesn't reason along the lines proposed by philosophers like Harman, for example: father says it's a dog, so father believes it's a dog, so there's (probably) evidence for it's being a dog, so it's (probably) a dog (see pp. 97–8). Her uptake is immediate. But human beings are intelligent and reflective creatures, and we are not bound to deliver the default response to what we perceive as informative speech-acts. Our responses *may* involve reasoning and they *may* go against the default. Moreover, being reflective, we have developed ways of describing, from the outside, so to speak, episodes of (informative) telling, together with the responses that the acts of telling may elicit. We now need to examine the second-order conceptual apparatus we have developed for these purposes and which we sometimes use to articulate what we ourselves are doing when we engage in the first-order activity as speakers or hearers.

To begin with, notice that the trained soldier who has been told to do something may be said to obey either the command or the commander. Something like this is also true with the person who has been told that P. So far I have spoken, with deliberate vagueness, of the hearer's "accepting" what she is told. This is clearly not the appropriate vocabulary to describe her response to her informant: she doesn't "accept" her informant, even when she accepts the proffered information. But it is more usual to use the vocabulary of *belief* here; and the hearer may be said both to believe the speaker who tells her that P, and to believe that P. The standard English way of describing a hearer's response to an informant when she accepts what she is told – the response that the speaker in performing this speech-act looks for – *is* to say that she believes the speaker: i.e. *believe* followed by the name of a person or a pronoun – "I believe him", "I believe John Doe, but not Mary Jane", and so on.

Some philosophers have written as if talk of believing a person were shorthand for talk of believing what the person has told us. But it is easily shown that this is not so. First, notice that I may utter indicative sentences in the hope that you will believe what those sentences say, but not in virtue of believing *me*. This book is a case in point. You are reading strings of indicative sentences that I have uttered (written), but my business is rational persuasion, and that is how I intend you to understand my utterances; I am not, for the most part, informing you of what is the case. If I am successful you will end up believing quite a lot of what I have said and what I myself believe, but only because I have convinced you, and not because you believe me. If you were to believe *me* you would be treating me as a source of authoritative pronouncements on the subject, someone who can *tell* you what is what. That is not my game. Secondly, there is the possibility of double bluff, noted earlier. If I think you are perpetrating a double bluff, I shall very likely end up believing what you tell me, but surely, since I suspect deceit, I shall not believe you.

What is it, then, to believe a person when they tell you something? As a first approximation, it is to accept what they say *on their say-so*. There is no solitarist backward reasoning from the speaker's assertion to the probability of what they say being true, *à la* Harman. One *can* reason in that way, but this is not the default response to the speaker's testimony, and it's a response that involves setting aside the social character of the act of telling. To believe a person when they tell you something is to respond to their speech-act in the manner fitting for speech-acts of that kind, by accepting the information that it contains; this is the natural, but not on that account the inevitable, response for one who has, in Fricker's phrase, "understood the speech-act for what it is". It also involves acknowledging the speaker's sincerity and her competence.

The acceptance of say-so is, as often as not, entirely unreflective. Think, again, of the way you accept the information on the labels of goods in the supermarket, in the telephone directory or on signposts. To be sure, in cases like these there is no obvious inform- ant to be believed. Still, the information was put there with the intention that it be available to anyone, and not to accept it would imply mistrust of whichever authorities put it there. At this level there is little, apart from the variety and sophistication of the information involved, to distinguish the way we humans uptake information from say-so and the way the bees do it from their fellows' dances. The process in both cases is unreflective, pretty well automatic. But unlike the bees we are conscious, articulate and reflective creatures, cognizant of the possibility of error, who have found ways of conceptualizing the process. Consequently, we are not locked into this primitive way of responding; our response may be conscious and may reflect our conceptualization.

To be consciously aware that say-so invites acceptance is also to be aware of choice. The natural response to an act of telling is to believe the speaker and thus accept what the speaker tells us. But as we become aware of our activity we also become aware that we are not *bound* to deliver this response. It can be withheld, and we can *disbelieve* the speaker. Realizing this, we can engage in Humean reflections about the credibility of our informant and their information. We then step out of the social game and adopt the stance of scientists or historians evaluating evidence.

Now suppose that our decision in a given case is not to believe the speaker. Here we choose to override the default. We may, nonetheless, think that she is sincere, although we doubt her competence. To have these thoughts is to make a distinction between the speaker's own individual perspective and what her perspective is a perspective on. She tells us that P and (since she is sincere) she thinks that P is the case, but in reality, so we think, P is not the case. This is the fundamental distinction that Plato insists must be preserved in his discussion of Protagoras' theory (see p. 29). The Protagorean abolishes this distinction and affirms that what seems to be true to each of us is true (for that individual) – period. When we recognize the possibility of a speaker's being wrong (it might even be ourselves) we thereby deny the primacy of individual viewpoints, which Protagoras affirmed. As we anti-Protagoreans conceive of it, what is conveyed through the speech-act of telling, when all goes well, is an objective view of how things really stand, independent of any individual's perspective. It *must* be independent of individual perspectives in order to be communicable. This point is catastrophically lost in solitarist interpretations of the reception of testimony like those of Harman, Goldman, Mellor and many others.

Knowledge

Our name for this objective view – what we might call, after the title of Thomas Nagel's (1986) book, "the view from nowhere" – is "knowledge". We have come to conceptualize the *social* act we are concerned with as the act of communicating *knowledge* from one person to another. A speaker telling someone that P, in performing that speech-act, lets it be understood that she knows that P; and the hearer, in believing the speaker, accepts what the speaker tells her as a bit of knowledge. In believing the speaker, she acknowledges the speaker's authority, however it may have been obtained, her competence to impart this knowledge to others.

It should not be thought that, in saying this, I am helping myself to an independently established concept of knowledge so as to explain what the business of telling other people things and of believing other people when they tell us things is all about. I claim, more radically, that the concept of knowledge is part of the very same conceptual package as telling and believing the speaker when we are told things. It is a concept that evolved in the conceptual scheme of human beings precisely to refer to what the business of telling is about, a concept that, perhaps, only appeared at a relatively advanced level of our development when we became capable of articulate reflection about our communicative practices. *Knowledge* just is our word for what a speaker communicates and a hearer accepts in episodes of telling. Or rather, it is those things in favourable circumstances; but, of course, *we* could not recognize as knowledge what our forebears were told and accepted as knowledge, half a millennium ago, when they were told that the earth was at the centre of the universe. This is disqualified as knowledge, in our eyes, because we do not accept it; we do not believe it is true. To accept what you are told in virtue of believing the teller is always to accept it as *objectively* true, independent of the individual perspective of the teller or of anyone else; the act of telling necessarily sets it in that objective frame. This is to accept it as knowledge. The reason why what is communicated through testimony is communicated as knowledge and not as belief is that, according to our ordinary conceptions, beliefs are relativized to individuals, while knowledge transcends individual points of view. When we say we agree with someone we are signalling a convergence of individual points of view. Knowledge, however, is essentially communicable, shareable, or, as John McDowell once put it, "contagious"; it is precisely what may be communicated through acts of telling. It thereby transcends individual points of view.

All this is bound into the concept of knowledge itself. This concept supports what I shall call the Principle of Communicability:

(PC) If a hearer (H) believes that a speaker (S) knows that P, then H believes that H knows that P

There is no parallel principle with respect to belief. It is not true that if H believes that S believes that P, then H (believes that H)

believes that P; H might accept that S believes that P but think that S is crazy to believe it.

The general point is this. In virtue of (PC), if I think that Percy knows that the cat is on the mat, I must think that I know it, too: that is how we conceive of knowledge. Knowledge which has been revealed is knowledge which has been made available to anyone to whom it has been revealed. When Percy tells me that the cat is on the mat he represents himself as knowing this, as having the (objective) truth of the matter; and this representation must be correct if he is really in a position to *tell* me, if he is really competent to perform this speech-act. For my part, in believing Percy – i.e. believing that he is not misrepresenting himself as a knower – I believe I know it, too. This is why, in testimonial transactions, content is, in Tyler Burge's phrase, preserved (see pp. 80, 135). Let us note, also, that in *believing that* I know that the cat is on the mat, necessarily I hold it true that the cat is on the mat, I *believe* it; consequently, this belief may inform my conduct. (Here it will be remembered that I surmise testimony evolved to supply our need for true, action-guiding beliefs.) My believing it in this case, however, is a consequence of my *believing that* I know it, of my having it in mind, as knowledge, in full consciousness; it is not entailed by my knowing it, as advocates of the tripartite forms of analysis would maintain. Their notion that an objective apprehension of reality can somehow be concocted out of what is essentially subjective, belief, is a great mistake. Our conception of knowledge, supporting (PC) as it does, is rooted in the practice of communication. What we conceive of ourselves as communicating has to be communicable in principle – i.e. it has to be conceived of as knowledge – and anything we regard as a matter of knowledge we think can be communicated by means of testimony.

Because we sophisticates have the concept of knowledge we may enlist it in a more sophisticated explanation of the transition in (TT); but it doesn't provide the most fundamental kind of explanation since the concept is itself a product of the practice. Thus, suppose that, as we are about to leave the house, I ask "Where's the cat?" What I need is a true belief on this matter, to guide my conduct effectively. If the cat is out, fine, but if she is in we'd better check the larder door. Being a sophisticate, however, I explicitly conceive of my goal in making this enquiry under the description *knowledge*; I conceive of myself as seeking knowledge about the cat's whereabouts. According to our conceptions, knowledge, unlike beliefs, is by its nature something we can hope to obtain from another person, in virtue of (PC). Now suppose that Percy replies "The cat is on the mat". Speaking thus in this context, he represents himself as one who is able to supply my want, in virtue of knowing the answer. In believing him, I accept this representation, I accept that he knows, and therefore, in virtue of (PC), I begin to suppose that I, too, know that the cat is on the mat.

(PC) describes a dynamic property of knowledge. It is logically possible that H does not know that P and S does know that P. Such states of affairs could hardly be more common, one person knowing what another person is ignorant of; it is what makes serious market-place enquiry possible. But if (PC) is correct, it is not possible that H herself should believe that this logically possible state of affairs obtains, even though S may believe that it does; H's belief that S knows that P forces the belief that H knows that P on to H. This may be disputed, by those who adhere to the kind of view about knowledge that is expressed in tripartite analyses. Thus Hintikka:

> There is an intermediate stage between your saying, justifiably, "I know" and my saying, justifiably, "*I* know," namely, my saying that I merely believe that you know but that I do not know myself. You may have the evidence but as long as you have not given it me, I do not "really" know.   (1962: 63)

Let us overlook the fact that Hintikka, like many other philosophers, seems to assume that the concept of knowledge is in the air only when the word *know* or some near equivalent is used; his point might be rephrased by speaking of your justifiably letting it be understood that you know and so on. Now he and I evidently have opposed intuitions here. Hintikka's intuition is that I must be able to justify any belief that is to count as knowledge. On my view, that "intuition" is the product of a particular philosophical culture. My intuition, of which (PC) is an expression, is more innocent; it reflects how we have come to think and speak, in an ordinary way, about the business of telling one another what is what and seeking information from one another.

Hintikka's stance may gain some plausibility from the way he describes the situation. I should not suppose that I definitely know that P if my belief that you know it is only tentative, more an inclination to believe that you know than unqualified belief. In such a case, one possibility would be that, tentatively believing that you know that P, I regard P as a candidate for knowledge and so seek out evidence for its truth that might satisfy me that there is a good chance of its being true. Now, for Hintikka this procedure will be interpreted as one in which I seek evidence that may tend to justify a belief that P and thus qualify it as knowledge. I interpret it differently. If my enquiries convince me that there is at least a realistic possibility of P's being true, then I may be happy, in the light of this ancillary evidence, to take your word for P. My enquiries serve to confirm my trust in your say-so, my inclination to believe you.

In a similar sort of situation, I might focus my enquiry differently, not on the credibility of P, but on your credibility. In this case, too, if I can satisfy myself that you are a reliable kind of informant, I may be happy to take your word for it. For Hintikka, however, no enquiry with this focus could have any bearing on the issue since in order to know that P, I myself must have evidence that bears directly on P, serving to justify a belief that P so as to make it knowledge. For Hintikka (and others, too), getting knowledge from testimony is a two-step process, getting a belief and also getting or working out some sort of warrant for it. My theory makes it a one-step process.

Let me conclude this section with some broad reflections about the road we have travelled. Right at the beginning we found Plato, in the *Republic*, proclaiming that there is a categorial difference between knowledge and belief. According to his way of thinking, to know P is to have gained access to the truth, to have attained a grasp on reality. To believe that P, on the other hand, is to have a more or less shadowy, and possibly completely mistaken, representation of what perhaps is the case. On this view, knowing P is altogether superior even to truly believing P (if that is not, for Plato, an oxymoron). When you know a thing, what is before your mind *is* the reality; but when you believe a thing, what is before your mind is at best an imperfect image of reality, a representation, but not the real thing. Knowing something is, perhaps, more like being acquainted with it, as in Russell's knowledge of things (see

p. 43). With belief, what is before your mind is only something like a proposition which, one may hope, represents reality more or less adequately. It cannot ever be right, therefore, to think of a person's knowing that P is a matter of their believing that P, when P is true, with good reason or whatever. What perhaps might happen is that a state of believing *metamorphoses* into knowledge when reason is fully engaged. That just possibly might be the thought behind the tenuous *Meno* account of knowledge and the fuller but failed account of the *Theaetetus*. Still, if that is the view, you could no more say that knowledge is a *species* of belief than that a butterfly is a kind of caterpillar.

Because Plato connects knowledge with reason so intimately, it seems that what one knows must be rationally attainable. So the necessary truths of mathematics are apt to be made a paradigm of what can be known. Among other things, this is what underpins Hume's preference for speaking of beliefs in the domain of matters of fact (see p. 43); however, if I am right about the connection between testimony and the concept of knowledge, this is an unfortunate preference in the context of his discussions of testimony. In any case, this high view of the nature of knowable truths is plainly at odds with our ordinary ways of speaking, and the philosophers of knowledge whose work has been dominant in recent years have all been happy to suppose that, in favourable circumstances at least, there can be such a thing as empirical knowledge, knowledge of ordinary matters of fact.

Those same philosophers have, for the most part, supposed that knowledge and belief are not, as at least *Republican* Plato thought, categorially different. Rather knowledge *is* a species of belief, namely, true belief with a special value-conferring feature, capable perhaps of securing it from the machinations of the Cartesian demon. These are the belief-theorists whose work we reviewed in Chapter 3.

Now, the theory I have just sketched doesn't fit neatly into any of these boxes. It places a high value on belief, certainly far higher than the value Plato places on it in the *Republic*. In a sense, on my view, *all* that matters is that we get beliefs that are true. This is what we need to live happy, successful lives; and, unsurprisingly as it seems to me, we have evolved in such a way that our capacity for getting true beliefs is roughly commensurate with our need for them. In particular, we have developed a way of getting them through the work of our fellow human beings so that we don't have to find out everything for ourselves *ab initio*. This possibility of testimonial communication causes us to think of the state it induces in a special way. When I accept that P on your say-so I cannot think that I merely *believe* that P. Believing is relativized to an individual point of view, but what I end up with by accepting your testimony isn't peculiarly *my* view of the facts; whatever it is, I got it from *you* and, in the context of testimonial transmission, I think of it as something that we both now have. We call it "knowledge". This conception of knowledge, the everyday conception as I maintain, is, in a way, quite Platonic. It is the conception of a kind of acquaintance with what objectively is the case. It is utterly different from beliefs, which are always subjective. For this reason it is wrong to think of knowledge as a *species* of belief: rather, in getting the beliefs we need through testimony, perforce we *recategorize* them as knowledge. Even in the event that they are false we categorize them as knowledge, although if we become aware of their falsity we shall, of course, withdraw that categorization.

I can imagine that someone might demand that I now explain how the concept of knowledge, on this interpretation, should be analysed; I have rejected the pattern of belief-theoretical analyses, which have become overwhelmingly fashionable during the past half century, so what sort of analysis do I propose? I don't propose any, nor could I. I can describe what we might call the knowledge-game. I can explain roughly how it is played (through social acts of testimony, in which the speaker tells the facts and the hearer accepts them on the speaker's say-so). I can point to the purposes it serves (the provision of true beliefs to match our practical needs and, it may be, our idle curiosities). I can mention some of the effects of playing the game (the creation of communities of knowledge and structures of mutual knowledge that enable advanced forms of collaborative undertakings). To demand, in addition to this, an *analysis* is to miss the point entirely.

The grammar of knowing and telling

The Principle of Communicability, (PC), can only apply to fully spelt out ascriptions of knowledge. If I believe that you *know that* the cat is on the mat I must, by (PC), believe I, too, know that the cat is on the mat. But if I believe that you *know where* the cat is, it by no means follows that *I* know where it is. As we have seen already (in our discussion of the Meno Paradox in Chapter 1), it is absolutely vital that we should have some way of ascribing specific bits of knowledge to others when we do not possess them ourselves. We do it with interrogatives. This is what makes focused enquiry and related practices possible. First, we have to be able to *identify* what we are ignorant of, if we are to be able to seek precisely that knowledge from other people. And, secondly, it may help both our own and other people's enquiries if we can identify potential sources of particular bits of knowledge that we do not possess ourselves; believing that you know where the cat is, I can ask *you* where it is in case I want to know, and I can direct Jane to ask *you* if I can't myself help directly with her enquiry. This is all essential to the communicative social practices that are dominated by the idea of knowledge.

Interrogatives are what enable us to identify the bits of knowledge that we lack and would like to possess; unlike the bees we can ask, "Where's the honey?" And we are able to identify potential sources of knowledge – experts, perhaps, or just people in a better position to know than we are – by attaching constructions introduced by interrogative words to the word *know*: other people may *know who*, *what*, *where*, *when*, and so on, even when we ourselves do not. It is important that *believe* does not tolerate these constructions. This creates a difficulty for the project of analysing knowledge in terms of belief. How, in the vocabulary of *belief* – *justified*, *reliably formed*, or whatever it may be, *belief* – can we represent such sentences as "Jane knows where the cat is"? Perhaps it can be done, although only at the cost of highly artificial circumlocution: "Jane has a true belief as to where (about where) the cat is", for example. That *know* does and *believe* does not tolerate these interrogative constructions is not an odd quirk of English grammar; it reflects that necessary distinction which we anti-Protagoreans make between private, subjective, individual points of view, on the one hand, and, on the other hand, apprehensions of how things objectively are.

These interrogative constructions are devices for referring to objective facts. Hence their usefulness in the making of enquiries and in identifying sources of information that may be made available to and shared with other people. This all connects with the most obvious logical difference between *know* and *believe*. If Tom knows *wh* (*who*, *what*, *where*, *when*, and so on), then any proposition that spells out what Tom knows in knowing *wh* will be true; there is no equivalent construction with *believe*. This carries through to *know-that*: if Tom knows that P, then it is the case that P; but *not*, if Tom believes that P then it is the case that P. Moreover, a speaker who asserts that Tom knows *wh* is thereby committed to believing that any proposition that spells out what Tom knows, in knowing *wh*, is true, and a speaker who asserts that Tom knows that P is thereby committed to believing that P herself; but there is no such commitment if a speaker asserts that Tom believes that P.

In the light of such facts as these, Zeno Vendler usefully adopted the term *factive* to describe the property that *know* has and *believe* lacks (Vendler 1979). In this terminology, *know* is a factive verb and *believe* is non-factive. The most reliable mark of factivity, as Vendler points out, is tolerance of *wh*-constructions. Now the verb *tell*, our standard word for the testimonial speech-acts we have been concerned with, appears to be a kind of hybrid in this respect. It tolerates *wh*-constructions and would, therefore, count as factive; if I say Jane told me where the key was, I am thereby committed to believing that the key was where Jane told me it was. If she told me that it was under the mat, and it turns out that it was not, it would not be correct to say that she told me where it was. But in this case I could truthfully report that she had told me that it was under the mat, even though it was not there and even though I believed it was not. In other words *tell-wh* appears to be factive, but *tell-that* is not. Vendler finds this puzzling. But it doesn't take much reflection to see that we need a "hybrid" word to describe our testimonial speech-acts. Human beings sometimes get things wrong, and they sometimes practise deceit. Consequently, we need to be able to describe their testimonial speech-acts without commitment to the truth of what they told us. But, of course, if we describe someone as telling-*wh*, using the construction that is, *par excellence*, factive, we are then committed to the thought that what they told truly was the case, even if we cannot spell it out for ourselves. Vendler's puzzlement would be dissipated if we attached the notion of factivity primarily to the *wh*-construction, where, I suggest, it belongs. We could then explain why the factivity is preserved in *know-that* but not in *tell-that*. In the former case the that clause spells out the fact referred to by the *wh*-clause; in the latter case the that-clause spells out the content of the telling.

Christopher Hookway has developed a theory about the use of know-*wh* constructions that contrasts intriguingly with mine (Hookway 1990: 192–214). His account is motivated by a desire to understand the concept of knowledge and his idea is that we might gain this understanding by reflecting on the use of sentences that employ the construction, "know-*wh*", too often neglected by philosophers of knowledge (his preferred formula is "know Q", but here I shall stick with mine). He and I agree that a central use for these sentences is to identify possible sources of information. If I need to know how many people are coming to the party it helps me to know that Percy knows how many are coming; I can then seek him out and ask him how many are coming. Hookway's idea is this: saying "Percy knows *wh*", in a context where I want to know *wh*, is tantamount to saying that Percy has a true belief on the matter about which I, as an enquirer, am curious. Hence, given that, as an enquirer, I want a true belief on the matter in question, it seems that Percy will be a suitable interlocutor. I shall be able to adopt for myself the belief that he expresses in reply to my question. So if, as we say, Percy knows how many are coming to the party and his reply to my question indicates that he believes that 25 are coming, I may infer that 25 *are* coming and act accordingly. Hookway's suggestion is that the underlying logic here is the logic of what he calls the "knowledge-inference":

(KI)   X knows *wh*
           X believes that P
           P is an answer to *wh*
           So: P

(Hookway 1990: 199, my terminology)

On my view this is a seriously mistaken account of how enquirers standardly get the true beliefs they want from the say-so of other people. But, of course, I believe that Hookway is right to offer an account that crucially engages the concept of knowledge in the process and I readily accept the claim, which for him is central, that "any case of true belief might non-metaphorically be described as knowledge if an appropriate context can be found", since in my view, at bottom, the institution of testimony evolved as a means of providing us with true beliefs that we may need in order to live our lives successfully. For all that, the so-called knowledge-inference has no part to play in the mechanism by which testimonial transitions are effected:

(TT) $$U_S P \rightarrow B_H P$$

On the contrary, the work is largely done by the hearer's recognition of the nature of the speech-act with which she is confronted.

This does not mean that there are *no* circumstances in which one might execute a knowledge-inference *à la* Hookway. Merely, if one does, the belief with which one ends up does not derive from accepting the speaker's utterance as testimony; the *mechanism* of testimony is not engaged although the concept of knowledge, and, with it, the Principle of Communicability are implicated. And, if I am right, we would not have the concept of knowledge at all, together with the principle, (PC), that it supports, if we had not developed the practice of testimony, so that even Hookway's inferential route from $U_S P$ to $B_H P$ *ultimately* depends on our having evolved the default mechanism I have described.

How can we envisage a knowledge-inference being used? Here is one possibility. Imagine that Percy, a master of wine and the leading expert on the wines of the Rhône Valley, is taking part in a competitive blind tasting. The object of the exercise is to deliver an informed opinion on the provenance and vintage of each of the wines tasted: that's the game. And those who are aware of this object will properly understand the competitors' utterances in this light, not as purveying information, but as expressions of opinion, expert guesses; and they will react accordingly, with an inclination to agree perhaps, but not with simple acceptance or belief of the speaker.

Now, like the other competitors, Percy offers more or less tentative judgements about most of the samples. But then, faced with one particular sample, he delivers a confident-sounding and quite specific opinion, which places it in the region of his special expertise. Even so, in this context, and in the absence of disclaimers that may, so to speak, detach the utterance from the context which otherwise indicates how it is to be taken, it is natural for an audience to receive his utterance as an expression of (confident) opinion and to respond appropriately, agreeing perhaps that it is highly likely in the circumstances that this sample is, indeed, Crozes Hermitage '95, or whatever. It would be wrong to describe someone who takes Percy's utterance in this way as accepting what they are told, or as believing him; such reactions require that the speaker is understood as telling or informing – uttering knowledge – and that is not the game.

Of course, things are not really quite so simple. In real life our understanding of one another is subtle and flexible, responsive to contextual nuance; and our actual speech-acts may be complicated in ways that defeat simple categorizations. Someone who was aware of Percy's expertise and registered the confidence of his utterance might think in the present case, "Well, *really* he's telling us" and accordingly believe him. Moreover, Percy may have deliberately modulated his response to elicit this reaction among his betting friends. It is not beyond his human powers that he should have meant different listeners to receive his utterance differently.

An audience that reacts as if his utterance were testimony – as if he were really telling them – will, if they believe him, end up thinking they know that the wine is Crozes Hermitage, and maybe act on this belief, placing their bets accordingly. The point is that if they do, it will not be through executing a knowledge-inference as described by Hookway, but by virtue of believing the speaker. Contrast the audience that is locked into the conventions of the wine-tasting game and, accordingly, receives Percy's utterance as an opinion, however confidently expressed. This audience might reason: "He thinks it's Crozes Hermitage and he knows more than anyone else about the wines from this region; I expect he's actually recognized it." Having reasoned thus, they, too, end up thinking they know what wine it is, and they do get there via a knowledge-inference; but this is only open to them because they do not treat Percy as *telling* them something – something to be accepted, if at all, on his say-so. They view Percy as having voiced a (confident) opinion. Hookway's knowledge-inference is one way of getting to the belief that P from someone's saying that P, a way that implicates the idea of knowledge and, with it, the Principle of Communicability; but it is not the way of *testimony*. In standard cases of the testimonial transmission of knowledge, there is no inference and no space for an inference. The uptake is immediate. In recognizing Percy as a knowledge-utterer, I take it that I, too, have the knowledge. This is what makes testimony, in Thomas Reid's words, a social as distinct from a solitary act. Inference is for solitary beings; we social creatures can often obtain the beliefs we need, to serve our practical ends, directly from one another, under the description *knowledge*, through our common understanding of the language we share and the facility it provides for telling one another what's what.

So, why do we value
7 knowledge?

It will be recalled that Plato, in the person of Meno, challenged us to say what it is about knowledge that makes us value it more highly than true beliefs. For creatures like us, mobile and active within the world, true beliefs are hugely important; as agents, we need them in order to achieve our goals, to avoid the impediments that might frustrate us, and to escape the dangers that otherwise might overwhelm us. The problem is, what more can we reasonably want? What has knowledge got that true beliefs lack?

Plato's suggestion, in the *Meno*, is that knowledge is somehow secured, tethered, whereas beliefs are apt to "run away". As we saw in Chapter 2, it is not easy to interpret Plato's meaning here. Perhaps the idea is that knowledge as such has some sort of built-in guarantee of truth, so that the person with knowledge can be confident that they are not wrong. At all events that seems to be an ideal that inspired a lot of later philosophy. The only problem is to work out how this happy state might be achieved. If the possibility that one might be wrong is thought to be a problem, it is hard to see how this approach helps. It only shifts the problem a step further back: how can you be sure that what you've got is knowledge? How do you know when you know? Descartes, it is true, thought that we could be absolutely sure that whatever we perceived very clearly and very distinctly was true. But could I not be wrong in thinking that I have a very clear and distinct perception of something?

The object, it seems, is to avert the possibility of being wrong. But why should we want to avert this possibility? After all, the fact that one *might* be wrong doesn't mean that one *is* wrong; it doesn't even mean that one cannot be reasonably sure that one is not wrong. And it doesn't mean that one may not be right most of the time. No human being can ever finally avert the possibility that she might be wrong on some particular matter, because we are all creatures of finite and corruptible capacities. The idea, to be found, for example, in Plato and Descartes, that lurking within us there is an infallible intellect whose deliverances can in principle be accessed with certainty, is fantasy. We cannot escape the human condition in virtue of which we are all liable to error. And if that is right, we may ask what use might creatures like us have for a concept – knowledge, conceived of as an infallible apprehension of truth – which in the nature of things could never be applied to us?

Well, perhaps it will be said, it could be some use. Perhaps it encapsulates an ideal that we can strive towards, even if, being what we are, we can never hope to attain it. Or perhaps we could go for a more modest account of knowledge as an achievable state that approximates to the ideal, the best cognitive state we humans can hope for, given what we are.

The difficulty with ideas like these is this. We have, well established in our language, words like *know* and *knowledge*, which, as we have seen, manifestly serve a series of useful linked purposes, purposes that are themselves linked with a valuable practice, viz., testimony. Moreover, other languages have equivalent words serving similar purposes; we are not talking about an odd quirk of English. It seems we operate with a certain concept, which is manifested whenever we use these words and is implicit whenever we engage in practices, like testimony, whose description requires them. But there is a huge mismatch between this serviceable concept that we all share and the concept that emerges from the sort of philosophical analyses that derive, for the most part, from philosophers' fear of scepticism and horror of being wrong. This latter concept requires that we attend to the state of the individual considered in isolation, whereas it seems the concept represented by our word *know* is standardly exercised in relation to our commerce with one another, in particular our engagement in social acts of communication.

It is now time to draw out our answer to Meno's Challenge. My suggestion is this: knowledge owes its value ultimately to the value

we rightly place on getting beliefs that are true. Because we need
true beliefs for the successful conduct of our lives, we need ways of
getting them. Our senses provide one way. Robinson Crusoe, alone
on his island, probably acquired a great many useful beliefs by
keeping his eyes and ears open and by careful experiment on what
he found. But he was lucky. With no one to guard his back and warn
him of approaching dangers he might have been killed by the wild
beasts. With no traditional lore to guide him he could easily have
poisoned himself. Being solitary he was cut off from a major and
vital source of true beliefs that could have ameliorated his life:
namely, his fellow human beings. We have evolved in such a way
that we are able to exploit the eyes and ears of other people to a
unique extent so as to obtain the (true) beliefs we want and need. At
bottom this is what testimony is *for*. Now, the concept of knowledge, on my account, developed so as to make articulate the underlying rationale of testimony. The value of knowledge, therefore, is
bound to the value of testimony, considered as a practice that can
provide us with beliefs we need and might not be able to obtain by
our own unaided efforts. Robinson Crusoe, once marooned, was
denied the benefits of testimony until the arrival of Man Friday. It
is a large part of what makes us distinctively human. In *The Web of
Belief*, Quine and Ullian remark that it is

> the first and greatest human device for stepping up the obser-
> vational intake. Telescopes, microscopes, radar and radio-
> astronomy are later devices to the same end.   (1978: 50–51)

Correct: testimony *is* valuable to us because it steps up our
observational intake. But it is misleading to classify it alongside
inventions like telescopes and microscopes. It isn't an add-on,
something that a primeval Edison might have invented to improve
our lot. Rather, it is something that has developed as our species
has evolved. It is not conceivable that creatures like us should lack
it. The practices associated with testimony – asking for information
on any topic under the sun, supplying information to others,
collaborating with others in shared enterprises that require that we
know what others know and they know what we know – are all
part of what it is to be human. So testimony matters to us not just
for its utility in stepping up the observational intake, but also

because it is an essential aspect of our social mode of being; it is partly responsible for our being the sort of creatures we are.

My idea, then, is this: the concept of knowledge enters our repertoire of concepts on the back of testimony, and it is a concept of something that owes its value ultimately to the value of testimony in our lives as a propagator of (mostly) true beliefs. To live in an environment where testimony is common is to live with the idea that there are other points of view besides our own, and a larger world only partially and imperfectly revealed to us in our own individual observations. You can see things I cannot see and, when you tell me about them and I accept what you tell me, they become part of my world as well as of yours; they become, for each of us, elements in a *common* world, which is independent of either of us. Through testimony we escape our own limited points of view to obtain the view from nowhere; this is what we call knowledge. We are not trapped in our private worlds; we can make sense of, and apply, the distinction that Protagoras rejected between how things seem to each of us individually and how they really are (see p. 28). Plato, in the *Republic*, maintained that knowing was the apprehension of realities that transcend the fluctuating appearances available from individual points of view: the domain of (mere) belief or seeming. If I am right, Plato was not so far off the mark. *Knowledge* is our word for the apprehension of objective (although not, on that account, transcendental or ideal) facts. It is no surprise that we should esteem it more highly than mere opinions, mere beliefs, which, by their nature, are subject to correction in the light of what is known.

It is better to know that P than merely to believe that P even when P is true. Notice (it's Plato's point against Protagoras) that you can only make the judgement that P *is true* if you have an idea of an objective world, against which the belief can be measured. We have that idea of objectivity in so far as we practise telling one another what is what, communicating what we know to one another. The existence of the objective world, which is the essential domain of knowledge, is presupposed in the judgement that a belief is true. So it is natural we should think of knowledge as superior to belief, even to *true* belief.

Now, it doesn't follow from the fact that we think of knowledge as valuable that our concept of knowledge is itself a *value*-concept, in the sense that any account we give of it should contain a reference to value, any more than it follows from the fact that food or sex is a good thing that the concept of food or sex needs to be explained in terms of value. But it is characteristic of the modern philosophy of knowledge to embed normative or evaluative notions in the analysis of knowledge. It's easy to see why. Any analysis that makes belief the core of knowledge will need a way of ensuring that the beliefs in particular instances are of good quality. Hence, on these accounts, to know that P is to believe that P, when P is true and in addition certain norms of rationality or acceptability have been satisfied.

I think this is wrong. If the concept of knowledge has arisen in the way I have suggested, in the course of our progressive conceptualization of those fundamental human practices that, at an advanced stage of our development, we have learnt to think of in terms of informative telling and the communication of objective truth, then knowledge just is the apprehension of objective truths. There is no space for a reference to norms *within* this conception of knowledge, although it may be hoped that we adhere to certain norms of responsibility in the way we engage in the practices that it supports: telling, teaching, reporting and so on. Unless we have some reputable basis that warrants our doing so, we *ought* not, by any of these means, let it be thought that we know that P. To assist and abet the spread of misinformation by means of testimony is wrong and tends to corrupt the human heritage of knowledge, which we all have an interest in protecting. We ought to *tell* or *teach* only what we know. This is where norms apply: to practice. The concept of knowledge itself, however, does not include normative elements. It is no more and no less than the conception of what is communicated and shared through such speech-acts as telling.

In this connection, it may be of some interest, finally, to compare my position with Edward Craig's (Craig 1986, 1990). Our theories have important features in common, but there is a fundamental difference, too. We both endorse the idea that the best way of achieving an understanding of the concept of knowledge is by trying to understand its role in human affairs, rather than by seeking an analysis of the necessary and sufficient conditions for its application to individual people. And we both think that the best illumination on its role will be obtained by examining the practice of testimony. Craig's guiding thought, or, as he puts it, his working hypothesis, is that the central use of the concept of knowledge is to flag *good*, or *approved* informants, so we can get our handle on the idea of knowledge by asking ourselves what we look for in a good informant. This provides him with all the material he needs for what he calls an "explication" of the concept. The point of an explication, as contrasted with an analysis, is roughly this: an analysis will list necessary conditions for the concept's correct application, but an explication will list something more like desiderata, which we may, in particular instances, be happy to waive. We can work out desiderata for ascriptions of knowledge in the light of our understanding of what we look for in a good informant. Belief, for example, will feature in the explication because someone who tells her hearers that P with conviction is more likely to inspire them with confidence and, to that extent, is a better informant than one who fails to inspire confidence.

In fact, the elements of Craig's explication pretty closely match elements of older style analyses: a good informant will normally be someone with a justified, true belief. The advantage of his approach is partly that it enables him to avoid the tedious business of endlessly refining definitions of knowledge to accommodate more and more recondite counter-examples; the lack of a desideratum is never, in itself, fatal. At the same time, it helps us to understand the attraction of the sorts of conditions on knowledge that have often been listed as necessary in traditional analyses.

For my part, I think this attractive-seeming strategy is mistaken, and I see no reason to think that the convergence of the elements in Craig's explication with components of more traditional analyses has any tendency to show that the explication is on the right track. I think that examining the notion of a *good* informant distracts us from the real meat. Better, in my view, to examine the notion of an *informant*, just *any* informant, or the human practice of informing, the business of testimony. The idea of knowledge is implicated in the practice as such; it is what supplies its rationale. It doesn't only come into view when the practice is well conducted.

The difference between us here is important. I remarked just now that unless you have some reputable basis that warrants it, you ought not perform any of the speech-acts whose use is to convey knowledge. If I were challenged to say what that involves, I should have to reply that you ought not to tell anyone that P (report that P, announce that P, remind someone that P and so on) unless you know that P yourself. Otherwise you misrepresent yourself as having knowledge when you do not. Knowledge, and knowledge alone, knowledge of objective fact, is what makes a teller competent. So we might say, a *good* informant that P precisely is someone who knows that P. But this idea doesn't give us an *independent* line on what knowledge is. The boot is on the other foot. The idea of knowledge can be usefully deployed in order to explain what it is to be an informant – period: to tell someone something just is to engage in a practice whose purpose is to propagate knowledge. But, of course, some speech-acts of telling fail in this objective; people lie and they can be honestly mistaken. A good informant is someone who *really* has the knowledge that she purports to have in virtue of producing a testimonial speech-act, knowledge of an objective fact which, in speaking thus, she is (puportedly) communicating to her hearers. The possession of knowledge is what *makes* an informant a good informant.

A guide to further reading

I have written this book without the distraction of footnotes. In this guide, I enlarge a little on the background to some of the chapters, comment on some points of difficulty, and provide pointers to further reading.

Chapters 1 and 2

These chapters are all about Plato. References to his works are given in the standard way by means of so-called Stephanus page numbers, which nearly always appear in the margins of both Greek and English editions of Plato. (*Stephanus* is the Latinized form of *Étienne* (French for *Stephen*), who was responsible for the first printed edition of Plato and several other ancient authors in the Renaissance.) There are numerous translations of Plato around. I have used those I am most comfortable with or have most ready to hand; they are listed in the References under *Plato*. I make special mention here of the Hackett Publishing Company's edition of the *Theaetetus*. This is the hardest of the Platonic works I deal with. This edition has a good translation by M. J. Levett and more especially a fine introduction (in effect a full-blown and advanced commentary) by Myles Burnyeat. Anyone who wants to unravel the harder knots in Plato's *Theaetetus* will find it helpful (Burnyeat 1990). *Plato's Meno in Focus*, edited by Jane Day (1994), combines a good translation with an introduction and a small collection of useful articles on the *Meno*. It hardly needs saying that the *Republic* is the most renowned of all Plato's works. Julia Annas's

Introduction to Plato's Republic (1981) is an excellent, middle-weight guide to this work. Nicholas White's *Plato on Knowledge and Reality* (1976) is a useful guide to all of Plato's writings on these topics. A fine, but heavier-weight guide, covering the same range, is I. M. Crombie's *An Examination of Plato's Doctrines, Vol. 11: Plato on Knowledge and Reality* (1963).

The Socratic doctrine that no one can act against what they know to be right, which I mention on p. 2, early became a focus of controversy; it is the starting point for subsequent discussions of what is often called weakness of will. The most famous (and difficult) examination of the topic in antiquity is Aristotle's in Book 7 of the *Nicomachean Ethics*. Donald Davidson wrote a classic article on the subject (Davidson 1980).

Plato's difficulties with the Theory of Forms, mentioned on p. 6, surface most notably in his *Parmenides*. The core of the problem lies in the convergence of two thoughts. First, he uses the idea of the Forms to explain our ability to use a predicate for lots of different particulars. For example, I call lots of different things beautiful, so I must have some idea of what it is to be beautiful, some inkling, that is, of the Form of Beauty. But secondly, Plato quite often thinks of the Forms as self-predicating: the Form of Beauty is itself beautiful, in fact, the only thing that is *perfectly* beautiful. Other things are beautiful only to the extent that they copy or resemble the Form. The combination of these thoughts generates what has become known as the problem of the Third Man. We explain how we are able to call Tom, Dick and Harry men by referring to the Form *Man*; but if the Form *Man* is itself a man (the Perfect Man) must there not be a super-Form, at a third level so to speak, to explain how the predicate applies to the Form as well as to Tom, Dick and Harry? Something has to give.

The discussion of enquiry in "Knowledge and enquiry", in Chapter 1 (pp. 9ff.), draws to some extent on my "Meno's Paradox" (Welbourne 1986a), which in turn refers to Nicholas White's "Inquiry" (1974). The most succinct and moving expression of the theory on which Plato draws to solve Meno's Paradox may be found in Wordsworth's "Ode: Intimations of Immortality From Recollections of Early Childhood":

Our birth is but a sleep and a forgetting;
The Soul that rises with us, our life's Star,
    Hath had elsewhere its setting,
      And cometh from afar;
    Not in entire forgetfulness,
    And not in utter nakedness,
But trailing clouds of glory do we come
    From God, who is our home . . .

In the *Meno,* the phrase *aitias logismos* has a crucial role in Plato's account of the difference between mere belief and knowledge (p. 24). This has received an odd variety of translations. I use the Penguin version: "working out the reason". The Greek is too succinct to be clear. In the eighteenth century Floyer Sydenham rendered it as "by deducing them [= the beliefs] rationally from their cause". Benjamin Jowett's classic nineteenth-century translation has "by the tie of the cause", but *logismos* could not possibly *mean* "tie". It is the *aitia* component that is translated as *cause*, or *reason* (in the sense of *explanation*); *logismos* means something like *rational calculation*.

Plato's difficulty with understanding how it is possible to have a false belief occupies a substantial section of the *Theaetetus* – 187d–200c; this material is hard, and the extensive literature about it is also hard. The subject is well discussed in Burnyeat (1990), which includes a good bibliography (pp. 65–123, 246–7).

Chapter 3

The classical source for the sceptical arguments, rediscovered in the sixteenth century, that stirred Descartes and Hume (pp. 37–8), is the voluminous writings of Sextus Empiricus (also published by Étienne). Some key texts are presented in Annas and Barnes (1985), with an excellent commentary, which relates them to later philosophical engagements with scepticism. Descartes's *Meditations* is the best source for his treatment of the subject. Hume's *Treatise*, Book 1, part 4, §§1 & 2 contains his subtle but very tricky discussion.

Descartes (p. 38) is usually associated with the sentence: "*Cogito ergo sum*". He says this in French in the *Discourse on the Method.*

In the *Meditations*, which actually *were* written in Latin, he uses the sentence translated in the text. It isn't obvious to me that they come to the same thing. Descartes's *Philosophical Letters* (1970: 83–4) gives an interesting slant on the matter.

Descartes's highly individualistic stance sits somewhat awkwardly with his apparent submission to the authority of the Catholic Church; in 1633, just four years before he published his *Discourse on the Method*, the Church had tried Galileo, another faithful Catholic, for heresy and had placed an embargo on the work in which he defended the idea of a sun-centred universe. In that year, Descartes resolved not to publish his own scientific treatise, *The World*. There is an excellent and compulsively readable account of these conflicts in Sobel's *Galileo's Daughter* (1999).

One relatively recent philosopher who has discussed the rationale of modern styles of analysis (p. 42) is R. M. Hare (1960).

There is a huge literature on Wittgenstein (pp. 42ff.), and in particular on his thinking about language, so it is hard to know what advice to give about further reading. Anthony Kenny (1973) writes enjoyably and with great clarity on this difficult topic. Ray Monk's (1990) biography is a fine and philosophically mature read. Zenon Stavrinides (1999) wrote a spirited attack on essentialism about knowledge in his doctoral dissertation, to which I am indebted.

It is contentious to call factual knowledge "propositional" knowledge (p. 44); Zeno Vendler thinks that propositions are the objects of belief only, whereas the objects of knowledge are *facts*. He strongly maintains, like Plato in the *Republic*, that there is a category difference between knowledge and belief, matched by a category difference in their objects (Vendler 1972: Ch. 5, and especially 1979: passim). I have learned a lot from Vendler; I take issue with some of his argument in Welbourne (1986b: appendix B).

The case of the lazy and diffident schoolgirl (p. 47) adapts a well-known example of Colin Radford's (1966).

The Gettier Problem (pp. 50ff.) is the focus of a vast amount of literature and all general accounts of modern epistemology have to deal with its fallout. Some of the earlier attempts to engage with the problem may be found in the numbers of *Analysis* immediately succeeding its first publication in that journal in 1963. Among recent general books I think the following are likely to be especially useful: Jonathan Dancy, *Introduction to Contemporary Epistemology* (1985) and Adam Morton, *A Guide through the Theory of Knowledge* (1997). Pappas and Swain's *Essays on Knowledge and Justification* (1978) collects some of the more influential articles on the topic.

Goldman is central to discussions of the causal theory of knowing. His original article (Goldman 1967) triggered some of the most productive developments in this part of philosophy. This article is collected along with some of the fallout (including some from Goldman) in Pappas and Swain (1978). I would add a beautifully written but little noticed piece (Robinson 1971), which has a quite different angle on the causal theory of knowledge and also anticipates some later developments in the field.

On tracking truth, Nozick (1981) is the essential text; Dretske (1971) develops a somewhat similar line. There's a good collection of articles on this important idea along with the relevant bit of Nozick in Luper-Foy (1987), and some astute criticism in Craig (1990).

The modern literature on knowledge abounds with "Ptolemaic" analyses (p. 67). They include Lehrer (1974: 21–3), Moser (1989: 254–5), Pollock (1987: 193) and Swain (1981: 194), all of which make considerable demands on the reader's stamina.

I first tried out the strategy of abandoning analysis and examining instead the role of the concept of knowledge in the lives of human beings in Welbourne (1986b: especially 71ff). This approach is also forcefully developed in Craig (1990).

A few other recent writers have sought in interestingly different ways to break the mould of entrenched tradition. At risk of seeming arbitrary, I single out for mention Haack (1993), who introduces a radically new angle on belief-theoretical approaches to knowledge and Williamson (2000), who develops an anti-belief-theoretical approach in great detail. Both these books are quite technical and make heavy demands on their readers.

Chapter 4

Karl Popper is the great champion of the idea of objective knowledge and the scourge of belief-theorists (Popper 1973). John

Hardwig has written a number of clear-headed articles on the implications of the practices of scientists for our idea of knowledge (1985, 1991). See also Adler (1994) and Webb (1993).

I first made made serious play with the idea of *commonable* knowledge in Welbourne (1986b: 1). I've begun to think the phrase is too outlandish for regular use, but it's still the best I can do by way of encapsulating the peculiar nature of knowledge in a single word.

Chapter 5

This chapter is largely about an important and revealing controversy centred on Hume's treatment of testimony. As noted, Hume in fact speaks of testimony as a means of obtaining beliefs rather than knowledge. In this context, however, nothing turns on the description given of whatever it is that the natural mechanism of testimony produces in a hearer. I attribute Hume's preference for the vocabulary of belief to his adherence to a high conception of knowledge, which restricts it to demonstrable and self-evident truths like those of mathematics (p. 79). It is of some interest that there is still a live question of whether knowledge of such truths can be obtained through testimony, even for those who recognize that knowledge of empirical truths can. See Williams (1972) and Coady (1981).

There are many books on Hume. Stroud (1977) has become, perhaps, the standard commentary. Mounce (1999) offers a beautifully lucid presentation of Hume's philosophy, which views him in much the same way that I do.

C. A. J. Coady is responsible for starting the modern controversy about Hume's treatment of testimony in Coady (1973). Coady (1992) is an excellent and wide-ranging discussion of testimony in general, which draws on the earlier article for its account of Hume. Leslie Stevenson examines the supposed opposition between Reid and Hume in an interesting way (Stevenson 1993). Some of the themes in this chapter are developed further in Welbourne (2001).

Chapter 6

I describe the theory introduced in this chapter as a *new* one. It is only fair to say that it appears to have affinities with a very ancient type of theory, although not one that has featured conspicuously in the tradition of Western philosophy. The idea that knowledge can be gained through understanding a speech-act is important in classical Indian philosophy. Some of the essays in Matilal and Chakrabarti (1994) explore this idea and it receives an extremely illuminating discussion in Ganeri (1999). I'd like to think that the convergence of two very different philosophical traditions on the same sort of idea is significant.

The notion of speech-acts of which I make substantial use is first adumbrated in Austin (1961) and more elaborately theorized in Austin (1962). This idea is Austin's most important contribution to philosophy and has been the subject of much subsequent discussion. Among the many general books about Austin, I have enjoyed Graham (1977) and Warnock (1989), written from rather different standpoints. Searle (1969) is a good general book about the theory of speech-acts.

The idea of the hearer's response to a speech-act, her uptake, is crucial to my account of testimony. This is not a topic that has been much noticed. It is, however, explored along with a number of related issues in an excellent monograph (Cohen 1992).

The section title "Telling the facts" (p. 101) is borrowed from Vendler (1979). I suspect I have learnt more from Vendler than from any other philosopher in this field, although I disagree with him rather radically on certain matters. I think he has not understood how it is possible to maintain both that the concepts of knowledge and belief are categorially different and that they can each have a role in the same bit of business: propagating beliefs by categorizing them as knowledge. See, for example, Welbourne (1986b: Appendix B).

I refer, both in this chapter and in Chapter 5, to Tyler Burge's notion of *content preservation* (Burge 1993). Curiously, although he sets it in the context of testimony he fails to understand its connection with knowledge; for him, content is preserved in testimony, but it is a *further* question whether what the hearer ends up with could be knowledge. That makes content preservation seem much more mysterious than it is.

References

Adler, J. F. 1994. "Testimony, trust, knowing", *The Journal of Philosophy* **XLI**: 264–75.

Annas, J. 1981. *An Introduction to Plato's* Republic. Oxford: Clarendon Press.

Annas, J.& J. Barnes 1985. *The Modes of Scepticism: Ancient Texts and Modern Interpretations*. Cambridge: Cambridge University Press.

Austin, J. L. 1961. "Other minds". In *Philosophical Papers*, J. O. Urmson & G. J. Warnock (eds), 44–84. Oxford: Clarendon Press.

Austin, J. L. 1962. *How to do Things with Words*, J. O. Urmson (ed.). Oxford: Clarendon Press.

Ayer, A. J. 1956. *The Problem of Knowledge*. Harmondsworth: Penguin Books.

Barnes, J. 1980. "Socrates and the jury", *Proceedings of the Aristotelian Society*, Supplementary Volume **LIV**: 193–206.

Berkeley, G. 1975. "A treatise concerning the principles of human knowledge". In *Berkeley: Philosophical Works*, M. R. Ayers (ed.). London: Dent [originally published 1710].

Burge, T. 1993. "Content preservation", *Philosophical Review* **102**: 457–89.

Burnyeat, M. 1990. *The* Theaetetus *of Plato*. Indianapolis, IN: Hackett Publishing Co.

Chisholm, R. M. 1966. *Theory of Knowledge*. Englewood Cliffs, NJ: Prentice-Hall.

Coady, C. A. J. 1973. "Testimony and observation", *American Philosophical Quarterly* **10**: 149–55.

Coady, C. A. J. 1981. "Mathematical knowledge and reliable authority", *Mind* **90**: 542–56.

Coady. C. A. J. 1992. *Testimony*. Oxford: Clarendon Press.

Cohen, L. J. 1992. *An Essay on Belief and Acceptance*. Oxford: Clarendon Press.

Cooper, D. 1987. "Assertion, phenomenology, and essence", *Proceedings of the Aristotelian Society*, Supplementary Volume **LXI**: 85–106.

Craig, E. J. 1986. "The practical explication of knowledge", *Proceedings of the Aristotelian Society* **LXI**: 211–26.

Craig, E. J. 1990. *Knowledge and the State of Nature: An Essay in Conceptual Synthesis*. Oxford: Clarendon Press.

Crombie, I. M. 1963. *An Examination of Plato's Doctrines, Vol 11: Plato on Knowledge and Reality*. London: Routledge & Kegan Paul.

Dancy, J. 1985. *Introduction to Contemporary Epistemology*. Oxford: Basil Blackwell.

Davidson, D. 1980. "How is weakness of will possible?". In *Actions and Events*, D. Davidson. Oxford: Clarendon Press [originally published in J. Feinberg (ed.) *Moral Concepts* (Oxford: Oxford University Press, 1969)].

Day, J. (ed.) 1994. *Plato's* Meno *in Focus*. London: Routledge.

Descartes, R. 1970. *Philosophical Letters*, A. Kenny (trans. and ed.). Oxford: Basil Blackwell.

Descartes, R. 1985. *The Philosophical Writings of Descartes* [2 volumes], J. Cottingham, R. Stoothoff & D. Murdoch (trans.). Cambridge: Cambridge University Press.

Dretske, F. 1969. *Seeing and Knowing*. London: Routledge & Kegan Paul.

Dretske, F. 1971. "Conclusive reasons", *Australasian Journal of Philosophy* **49**: 1–22 [reprinted in G. Pappas & M. Swain (eds) *Essays on Knowledge and Justification* (Ithaca, NY: Cornell University Press, 1978)].

Fricker, E. 1987. "The epistemology of testimony", *Proceedings of the Aristotelian Society*, Supplementary Volume **LXI**: 57–83.

Gale, R. (ed.) 1968. *The Philosophy of Time*. London: Macmillan.

Ganeri, J. 1999. *Semantic Powers: Meaning and the Means of Knowing in Classical Indian Philosophy*. Oxford: Clarendon Press.

Gettier, E. 1963. "Is justified true belief knowledge?", *Analysis* **23**: 121–3.

Goldman, A. 1967. "A causal theory of knowing", *Journal of Philosophy* **64**(12): 355–72 [reprinted in G. Pappas & M. Swain (eds) *Essays on Knowledge and Justification* (Ithaca, NY: Cornell University Press, 1978)].

Graham, K. 1977. *J. L. Austin: A Critique of Ordinary Language Philosophy*. Hassocks: Harvester Press.

Haack, S. 1993. *Evidence and Enquiry*. Oxford: Basil Blackwell.

Hardwig, J. 1985. "Epistemic dependence", *Journal of Philosophy* **82**: 145–62.

Hardwig, J. 1991. "The role of trust in knowledge", *Journal of Philosophy* **88**: 693–708.

Hare, R. M. 1960. "Philosophical discoveries", *Mind* **LXIX**: 145–62.

Harman, G. 1990. *Skepticism and the Definition of Knowledge*. New York: Garland Publishing.

Hintikka, J. 1962. *Knowledge and Belief*. Ithaca, NY: Cornell University Press.

Hookway, C. 1990. *Scepticism*. London: Routledge.

Hume, D. 1932. *The Letters of David Hume*, J. Y. T Grieg (ed.). Oxford: Clarendon Press.

Hume, D. 1975. *Enquiries Concerning Human Understanding and Concerning the Principles of Morals*, 3rd edn, L. A. Selby-Bigge (ed.), P. H. Nidditch (rev.). Oxford: Clarendon Press [reprinted from posthumous edition of 1777].

Hume, D. 1978. *A Treatise of Human Nature*, 2nd edn, L. A. Selby-Bigge & P. H. Nidditch (eds), P. H. Nidditch (rev.). Oxford: Clarendon Press [originally published 1739–40].

Kaplan, M. 1985. "It's not what you know that counts", *Journal of Philosophy* **82**: 350–63.

Kenny, A. 1973. *Wittgenstein*. London: Allen Lane, The Penguin Press.

Lehrer, K. 1974. *Knowledge*. Oxford: Clarendon Press.

Locke, J. 1975. *An Essay Concerning Human Understanding*, P. H. Nidditch (ed.). Oxford: Clarendon Press.

Luper-Foy, S. 1987. *The Possibility of Knowledge*. Totowa, NJ: Rowman & Littlefield.

Matilal, B. K. & A. Chakrabarti (eds) 1994. *Knowing From Words: Western and Indian Analysis of Understanding and Testimony*, Synthese Library Vol 230. Dordrecht: Kluwer.

Mellor, D. H. 1990. "Telling the truth". In *Ways of Communicating*, D. H. Mellor (ed.), 81–95. Cambridge: Cambridge University Press.

Monk, R. 1990. *Ludwig Wittgenstein: The Duty of Genius*. London: Jonathan Cape.

Morton, A. 1997. *A Guide Through the Theory of Knowledge*, 2nd edn. Oxford: Basil Blackwell.

Moser, P. 1989. *Knowledge and Evidence*. Cambridge: Cambridge University Press.

Moser, P., D. H. Mulder & J. D. Trout 1988. *The Theory of Knowledge*. Oxford: Oxford University Press.

Mounce, H. O. 1999. *Hume's Naturalism*. London: Routledge.

Nagel, T. 1986. *The View From Nowhere*. Oxford: Oxford University Press.

Nozick, R. 1981. *Philosophical Explanations*. Oxford: Clarendon Press.

Pappas, G. & M. Swain (eds) 1978. *Essays on Knowledge and Justification*. Ithaca, NY: Cornell University Press.

Plato 1956. *Protagoras and Meno*, W. K. C. Guthrie (trans.). Harmondsworth: Penguin Books.

Plato 1990. *The* Theaetetus *of Plato*, M. Burnyeat, with Plato's *Theaetetus*, M. J. Levett (trans.), M. Burnyeat (rev.). Indianapolis, IN: Hackett Publishing Co.

Plato 1992. *Republic*, G. M. A. Grube (trans.), C. D. C. Reeve (rev.). Indianapolis, IN: Hackett Publishing Co.

Pollock, J. 1987. *Contemporary Theories of Knowledge*. London: Hutchinson.

Popper, K. 1973. *Objective Knowledge: An Evolutionary Approach*. Oxford: Clarendon Press.

Quine, W. V. & J. S. Ullian 1978. *The Web of Belief*, 2nd edn. New York: Random House.

Radford, C. 1966. "Knowledge – by examples", *Analysis* **27**(1): 1–11.

Reid, T. 1863. "Essays on the intellectual powers of man". In *The Work of Thomas Reid*, 6th edn, W. Hamilton (ed.). Edinburgh: Maclachlan & Stewart.

Reid, T. 1970. *An Inquiry into the Human Mind*, T. Duggan (ed.). Chicago, IL: University of Chicago Press.

Robinson, R. 1971. "The concept of knowledge", *Mind* **LXXX**: 17–28.

Russell, B. 1959. *The Problems of Philosophy*. Oxford: Oxford University Press.

Ryle, G. 1949. *The Concept of Mind*. London: Hutchinson.

Searle, J. R. 1969. *Speech Acts*. Cambridge: Cambridge University Press.

Sobel, D. 1999. *Galileo's Daughter*. London: Fourth Estate.

Stavrinides, Z. 1999. *The Question: "What Is Knowledge?"*, PhD dissertation, Department of Philosophy, University of Leeds.

Stevenson, L. 1993. "Why believe what people say?", *Synthese* **94**: 424–51.

Strawson, P. F. 1952. *Introduction to Logical Theory*. London: Methuen.

Strawson, P. F. 1959. *Individuals: An Essay in Descriptive Metaphysics*. London: Methuen.

Stroud, B. 1977. *Hume*. London: Routledge & Kegan Paul.

Swain, M. 1981. *Reasons and Knowledge*. Ithaca, NY: Cornell University Press.

Thurber, J. 1954. *The Thurber Carnival*. Harmondsworth: Penguin Books.

Vendler, Z. 1972. *Res Cogitans*. Ithaca, NY: Cornell University Press.

Vendler, Z. 1979. "Telling the facts". In *Contemporary Perspectives in the Philosophy of Language*, P. A. French, T. E. Ueling & H. K. Wettstein (eds), 220–32. Minneapolis, MN: University of Minnesota Press.

Walsh, W. H. "Knowledge in its social setting", *Mind* **LXXX**: 321–36.

Warnock, G. J. 1989. *J. L. Austin*. London: Routledge.

Webb, M. O. 1993. "Why I know about as much as you: a reply to Hardwig", *Journal of Philosophy* **90**: 260–70.

Welbourne, M. 1979. "The transmission of knowledge", *Philosophical Quarterly* **29**: 1–9.

Welbourne, M. 1986a. "Meno's Paradox", *Philosophy* **61**: 229–43.

Welbourne, M. 1986b. *The Community of Knowledge*. Aberdeen: Aberdeen University Press [reissued by Ashgate Publishing in 1993].

Welbourne, M. 1987. "What is knowledge? The structure of the argument in Plato's *Theaetetus*", *Cogito* **1**(1): 12–14.

Welbourne, M. 1989. "A puzzle about telling", *Philosophy* **64**: 175–85.

Welbourne, M. 2001. "Is Hume really a reductivist?", *Studies in the History and Philosophy of Science* (forthcoming).

White, N. 1974. "Inquiry", *Review of Metaphysics* **28**: 289–310.

White, N. 1976. *Plato on Knowledge and Reality*. Indianapolis, IN: Hackett Publishing Co.

Williams, B. A. O. 1972. "Knowledge and reasons". In *Problems in the Theory of Knowledge*, G. H. Von Wright (ed.), 1–11. The Hague: Martinus Nijhoff.

Williamson, T. 2000. *Knowledge and its Limits*. Oxford: Oxford University Press.

Wittgenstein, L. 1953. *Philosophical Investigations*, G. E. M. Anscombe (trans.). Oxford: Basil Blackwell.

Wittgenstein, L. 1958. *Preliminary Studies for the "Philosophical Investigations"*, the "Blue and Brown Books". Oxford: Basil Blackwell.

Index